Working in Innocence Programs:

Everything You Always Wanted To Know About Innocence Work But Were Afraid To Ask

By

Sarah A. Mourer

VANDEPLAS PUBLISHING, LLC
UNITED STATES OF AMERICA

Working in Innocence Programs: Everything You Always Wanted To Know About Innocence Work But Were Afraid To Ask

Mourer, Sarah A.

Published by:

Vandeplas Publishing, LLC – January 2013

801 International Parkway, 5th Floor
Lake Mary, FL. 32746
USA

www.vandeplaspublishing.com

ISBN 978-1-60042-184-6

<u>Working in Innocence Programs</u>:

Everything You Always Wanted To Know About
Innocence Work But Were Afraid To Ask[1]

By

Sarah A. Mourer[2]

---

[1] *See* EVERYTHING YOU ALWAYS WANTED TO KNOW ABOUT SEX (BUT WERE AFRAID TO ASK) (Rollins-Joffe Productions 1972). Starring Woody Allen.

[2] Sarah Mourer is an Associate Professor of Clinical Legal Education at the University of Miami School of Law. Professor Mourer is the Director of the Miami Law Innocence Clinic and Director of the Miami Law Death Penalty Clinic. Professor Mourer would like to thank Craig Trocino, Sam Kugbei, Liz Jansky, Justin Brooks, Keith Findley, Rob Schehr, Seth Miller, Beth Gordon-Rico, Jessica Lee, Brenda Schamy, Sarah Cardone, Charles Mourer Calli, David Freitas, and Mary Mourer for their support in the writing of this book. Professor Mourer would also like to thank all of the members of The Innocence Network for consistently providing her with guidance and support.

Dedicated to the students of the Miami Law Innocence Clinic who inspire me every day

Contents

Chapter One

Introduction: Who Should Read this Book and Why?

This little book is for students and directors of innocence programs. If you are not a student or director put this book down. If you are a student, welcome and read on. If you are a director of an innocence program, you might also read this book for a couple of reasons. First, if you assign this book to your incoming students, they will hit the ground running. Second, this book provides insight into how other programs operate successfully.

If you are a student reading this book, chances are you are either already signed up for an innocence program, thinking of applying to work in one, or have way too much time on your hands.[3] If you are thinking of doing innocence work or already doing it, this book is especially for you. It is a guide for students who work in innocence programs whether for academic credit, on a volunteer basis, or for pro bono hours. The information provided in this book is generalized so it should send you in the right direction no matter what sort of innocence program you participate in. This book should supplement the materials your director or supervisor provides to you in your innocence program.

Before we launch into the nuts and bolts sections, any book for students thinking about innocence work would be remiss not to discuss why you want to take on the grief and heartache of others in an innocence program in the first place. If you have already signed on, depending on how you feel after reading this book, we may need to talk about how you can back out with a plausible story to your director or professor, possibly something involving a very contagious rash. In all seriousness, while innocence work is rewarding, it will require your heartfelt commitment and hard work.

This book will be honest with you. Innocence work is hard. You probably want to join an innocence program to help exonerate an innocent person. Perhaps, you envision yourself as the hero getting that tearful courtroom hug of gratitude from a client who was wrongfully behind bars for decades and watching his family rush into his arms after you managed to get him exonerated. Now, let's rewind three to five, or often even more years. What kind of work led up to those hugs?

[3] If you do not meet criteria 1 or 2 – go study.

You will have to read literally thousands of pages of transcripts, and that is only the beginning. To be candid, this part of innocence work can be unexciting, yet it is crucial to obtaining an exoneration. Doing this work takes endurance, stamina and a lot of coffee.[4]

So you say you are in? This book will discuss how to best prepare yourself for distinction in your performance in an innocence program. If you know well in advance that you plan on applying to an innocence program, this book will answer many of your questions including, what are the best classes to take and what are the best skills to have? This book will also provide you with invaluable tips. One important tip before you begin the program is to get as much sleep as possible. The other tips are listed in Chapter Four.

Working with an innocence program is real. Your clients are real human beings. Although this is scary, it can be made less scary. This book will discuss how to cope with life and death issues, while maintaining a personal life. We will also discuss how to feel good about what you are doing and how to do it with excellence. In an innocence program, you may be dealing closely with individuals who may or may not have committed disturbing crimes. In any event, the allegations will be disturbing, and even if your client is innocent, the crime itself is likely to be gruesome and upsetting to you. This book will provide advice for discussing, investigating, and dealing with distressing and graphic crimes. You may already have noticed that this book uses humor in parts. Humor can be used as an outlet to help you manage events or traumatic conditions that your clients and victims have had to endure. As the attorney, you may even suffer some secondary trauma. Use of humor is helpful only if the humor is used appropriately. This book itself is an example of the appropriate use of humor. We will later discuss how to keep humor within proper boundaries.

This book will also provide you with: screening techniques for reviewing applications or letters received by your program, some common screening criteria and why they are important, some of the major causes of wrongful convictions and how to spot them, some avenues of innocence investigation and how to get started,

---

[4] Warning: innocence work may cause caffeine addiction. Please disregard if you are past your first year in law school because you are likely already caffeine addicted. In all seriousness, please be careful regarding your caffeine intake. If you find yourself drinking caffeinated beverages or taking caffeine pills, you may need to do a self-check and ask yourself if you are taking on too much work. Plus, caffeine withdrawal headaches are the worst!

and a brief overview of the remedies that might be available to you for a claim of actual innocence. We will also go over some of the skills needed to do well in an innocence program, such as interviewing witnesses, clients, and family, and we will provide you with sample forms that should help you with evidence requests and writing letters to clients, agencies, and other individuals.

Lastly, in Chapter Thirteen, this book will discuss documenting your cases. You will graduate (presumably) and your clients will be left behind to be assisted by new students. Therefore, tracking and documentation is one of the most important things you will learn to do in the innocence program. Documentation and tracking are skills that you will need in any area of law and in any law firm. All cases, regardless of the type of law you eventually practice, must be thoroughly documented. In fact, an innocence program should run much like a small law firm. Therefore, many of the skills you will acquire while practicing in an innocence program will transfer to any legal job you choose in the future.

Innocence programs with students involved are successful because students are motivated, enthusiastic and smart. Use of this book should ensure that you are well prepared and heading in the right direction on your cases. Keep in mind, however, this book should never take the place of directions or guidance given to you by your supervisor, director or professor. Every director has his or her own style of teaching. It is important that you respect your director's style and follow his or her lead. Also realize that each program is different. This book may list procedures that differ in form from your program. It is important to always follow your program's specific procedures. This book is meant to supplement your other materials by giving you a head start and a little help when you need it.

PART I: WHAT DO I WANT? HOW WILL I DO IT?

Chapter Two

What Will I Do in an Innocence Program, Project or Clinic?

An innocence program is generally a program operating for the purpose of identifying and exonerating innocent prisoners. There are a variety of models for innocence programs, run in many disciplines, including criminology, social sciences, psychology, and journalism. A group of innocence programs, collectively called The Innocence Network, span from the Midwest of the United States the Netherlands. Only members of the Innocence Network may call themselves "Innocence Projects." The first Innocence Project was established at New York's Cardozo Law School in 1992[5].

Innocence programs should aspire to gain membership into The Innocence Network. The Network (as we will call The Innocence Network hereafter) provides Innocence Projects with privileges and benefits that make obtaining exonerations much more likely. For example, Innocence Projects benefit from The Network's many different internet "listservs" which enable Projects to send any question via the internet to the many other Projects doing the same work.

Innocence programs usually have a set of criteria that an inmate must meet before a program will investigate his or her case. Most programs also require that the inmate complete an application,[6] primarily so that you, or other innocence program staff, can make a fully informed decision as to the suitability of the case for further investigation. On occasion, a client's case can be denied based on the

[5] Although The Cardozo Law School was the first "Innocence Project", it was not the first program to work to identify and exonerate wrongfully convicted prisoners. Other such programs existed prior to it and many other programs that are not a part of the network exist today. It is believed that the very first program to ever do innocence work was Centurion Ministries in New Jersey. The Miami Law Innocence Clinic is a member of The Network as are many Innocence Programs that choose not to use the word "Project" in their title.

[6] *See* Appendix for a sample of an application similar to one many innocence programs use.

inmate's letter alone. This occurs only when the letter makes it abundantly clear that the case does not meet the program's criteria. Sometimes, the letter will indicate that the crime was committed in another state, in which case your innocence program is likely to refer that letter to the innocence program in that state.

Nearly every innocence program has financial problems. In part, this is why there must be screening criteria. Innocence programs are flooded with letters from inmates wanting you to get them out of jail or prison; yet no innocence program, in my awareness, has the funding to hire enough staff to investigate and assist in every claim. Further, inmates do not always claim that they are innocent. Their issues can range from innocence claims such as asserting that they were on the opposite side of the world at the time of the crime, to "I did it but…." claims like declaring that he didn't mean for the victim to die when he strangled her, that he was just mad, and he would like you to get his sentence reduced based on lack of intent. In large part, this is why most innocence programs require that the applicant is asserting that he or she is actually innocent. Actually innocent means that the inmate is claiming that he had nothing to do with the crime at all: someone else committed the crime, or there was no crime at all (e.g., a death was not a homicide, but the product of natural causes or an accident). Some innocence programs do not require actual innocence. These programs should technically be called "wrongful convictions programs".

A full application is often necessary to ensure that the program does not deny help to an innocent person. This is a major concern for any program, and is the reason many programs take on too many cases and overwork themselves. This is a difficult balance for a program to reach. Enormous backlogs can be created while the students and attorneys investigate every nook and cranny until the program can be sure of the client's guilt or innocence. Discovering innocence takes extensive investigation, and you must always be clear with your professor if you begin to feel overworked to the degree that you are unable to perform adequate investigation or feel pressure to close cases. A backlog is a natural part of an innocence program. It is similar to the sign in sheet or plaque on the wall of a doctor's office waiting room that says *the doctor takes his time with all patients and he will take his time with you too, so he apologizes for your three hour wait.* You do not want that doctor to overlook another patient's restless leg syndrome (a real illness, and a painful one too) or serious illness because he is in a hurry to get to the crowded angry waiting room. If you have a time limitation in your jurisdiction, you may need to look through your backlog to ensure that no deadlines are passing; short of that, your obligation is to your current clients.

Innocence programs often have students screen and investigate cases. Screening involves reading the inmate's application thoroughly and assessing whether the inmate's circumstances meet the program's criteria. Some programs use intake coordinators for the initial application screening, which helps to avoid large backlogs of cases. Investigation of an innocence claim involves many things that will be discussed further in Chapter Nine. Some examples are: interviewing your client and client's family, interviewing any witnesses your client identifies, reading all court records and transcripts, contacting your client's previous lawyers and prosecutors, and searching for biological evidence.

If investigation leads to a viable motion for post-conviction relief in your jurisdiction, then you (if permitted by your supervisor) or you and your partner (if you are working in teams) might write the motion and file it. In some jurisdictions, you might also argue the motion. Some states and some supervisors allow students who become certified legal interns (CLI) to speak in court as a lawyer would, as long as they are supervised. Although the CLI rules may vary for each state, almost every state has some form of the rule. Make sure you are aware of the rules in your state, because many states require prerequisites that could take months to complete.

Innocence programs[7] differ in structure depending on many factors. Usually, the program's structure is determined by its source of funding. Many innocence programs are at least partially funded and housed by law schools. Others function solely on funding from grants and may or may not involve students. In addition to identifying and rectifying wrongful convictions, innocence programs that are based in law schools have the added mission of providing the students with a high quality academic experience. This balancing act will be discussed further. Your client must always come first; however, your director or supervisor must also ensure you are learning and performing well.

Before you apply to work or volunteer in an innocence program, find out what your role will be and assess the quality of the program. Here are some questions to ask the director or appropriate representative:

---

[7] The term "innocence program" will be used to refer to an organized system run by people for the purpose of exonerating innocent individuals.

1) If you find grounds for a motion, will you be permitted to write the motion?
2) What training will you get other than this book?
3) Will you be allowed to speak to your clients?
4) Will you be allowed to travel to visit your clients?
5) What are the rules in your state to become "certified" and be permitted speak in court?
6) If you were certified, would the director allow you to argue the motion?
7) What happens if you are convinced of a person's innocence but he does not meet the program's screening criteria?
8) What happens if the director wants to deny a case but you are convinced of the person's innocence?
9) What resources does the program provide to assist students in these situations or any other problems?
10) Ask to see the program's written mission statement.
11) What prerequisites are there? If there are none – why?
12) Will they interview you? If no – why?
13) Will they look at your transcript, GPA, writing sample? If no – why?
14) Is this program part of the National Network of Innocence Projects?

As discussed, membership in the Network provides innocence programs with valuable benefits. A program that has been unable to obtain membership in the Network may need to revamp some of its procedures; this book could assist in that endeavor. If you decide that your nearest innocence program is not right for you or you cannot locate a network affiliated program, go to http://www.innocencenetwork.org/members for a list of all National Network Innocence Projects.

Chapter Three

Do I Really Want To Do Innocence Work?

This is not an easy question to answer. The endeavor of rescuing an innocent person from a life in prison, or from dying in prison, is by any standard, a commendable and worthy enterprise. It is not, however, for everyone and there is no shame in saying that innocence work is not for you. You can still enrich the community in many other ways that do not involve dangerous criminals and abhorrent crimes such as rape or murder of a child. Some suggestions are: defending the homeless, human rights policy work, children's rights, or immigration programs. Innocence work will probably not lead you to a well-paying job, only to self-satisfaction, fulfillment of your intrinsic values, and chronic sleep deprivation.

Be aware that once you are engaged in innocence work, people's lives literally rest upon your work, upon your ability to cope with multiple tasks at once, and concentrate on extended tedious work. You will need the capacity to be caring and optimistic towards others even when you feel powerless, and even when you may be shocked by the crimes your clients are accused of committing. Given the number of letters and applications innocence programs receive, finding a case with a possibility for exoneration is a relatively rare thing. It may be said that you will be looking for a needle in a haystack. You must view each piece of hay passed as one piece of hay closer to the needle. Needles are there and you can find one, but there is a lot of hay to sift through. It is crucial that you view each passing case or each denial of a case as one of the following: one step closer to success, a learning experience, or simply as attention given to a lonely prisoner. For those who prefer chocolate to hay, a better analogy might be finding the golden ticket from Willy Wonka. You could view each passing case as a chocolate bar consumed to maintain the enthusiasm and fortitude needed to find the golden tickets we know are there: the innocent prisoners out there who need you. In short, you must have responsibility, endurance and genuine commitment. Nothing less will do.

Some questions to ask yourself before deciding to apply to an innocence program (in addition to the issues discussed above) are:

1. Will my schedule allow me to commit the time necessary to fully and completely perform a first-rate job in the innocence program?
2. Can I feel compassion for all my clients, and will I work hard for those clients who are ultimately denied because the program concludes, or you conclude, that the client is guilty?
3. Can I treat inmates who may have committed atrocious crimes civilly and kindly?
4. Can I respect other students' or colleagues' views when they differ in opinion regarding the guilt or innocence of clients incarcerated for heinous crimes?
5. Can I commit myself to working long hours on tedious jobs like outlining long trial transcripts for the cause of identifying innocent prisoners?
6. Can I be sure that I will remain committed to identifying innocent prisoners and pursuing an exoneration even when I go a long time without finding one, even when I may never find one?
7. Do I fully realize that an innocence program's work is the representation of real people, not a mere academic exercise, and with that work comes the related responsibilities?
8. Given that I will be representing real people in real cases, am I ready to handle issues that arise at inconvenient times like holidays and vacations?
9. Do I have the ability to work as a team and resolve conflict when it arises with integrity and maturity?
10. Am I able to ask any questions necessary – and some are very tough to ask - to do an exemplary job?
11. Am I able to prioritize my tasks, seek assistance when needed, and never take on too much work to be an effective advocate?
12. Do I have the ability to conduct thorough and accurate legal research?
13. Can I demonstrate respect toward everyone within the profession including my adversaries, judges, prosecutors, staff, and all clients?
14. Can I demonstrate sensitivity to any race, cultural diversity, disability, or any issues that may offend me?
15. Can I be punctual to court and class or any other appointment?
16. Can I submit all assignments in a timely fashion?
17. Will I put thought, reflection and effort in all that I do within the program?

18. Can I be a reflective practitioner? Can I reflect on how my participation in the program affects me as a person and what it means for me personally?
19. Will I be committed, enthusiastic, and professional?
20. Finally, make a list of reasons you wish to participate in an innocence program. Be honest with yourself. Have you heard that all students in these programs get good grades? Do grades play a big role in your desire to participate? Do you think it will be exciting? What personal or academic needs do you believe an innocence program will satisfy for you?

That sounds like a lot of questions and requirements. I said this book would be honest. Many programs will admit a student to the program even if the above questions are not addressed and considered. I suggest, however, that your experience in an innocence program without all of the above standards may hurt both you and your clients. Many innocence programs are graded and will have grading criteria that look very similar to the above questions. You may not know the program's grading criteria until you are already in the program. Thus, I highly suggest you contemplate these questions before you make your decision or submit an application.

Chapter Four

How to Prepare Yourself for Working in an Innocence Program

First, reconsider... are you still here? Good, now go back to Chapter Three and reread the twenty questions. Still here? Great. You have passed the *innocence program commitment test*. Congratulations. This short chapter is intended for those of you who are not yet in an innocence program, those looking for more information or for those simply interested in how to learn more about innocence work. However, some of the tips in the list below may be thought provoking for anyone interested in the innocence cause even if you are already participating in an innocence program.

You will need to pick and choose what information in this section is applicable to you. You could be my fourteen year old son who already knows that he wants to be in an innocence program someday and already does my power-points.[8] More likely, you are in your first or second year of law school and would like to do the innocence clinic in your third year, or you are already in an innocence program. To prepare yourself for an innocence program or do well in one, you must consider the skills that you will be using.

First and foremost, you will need a firm grasp of post-conviction law. Many programs require a post-conviction class as a co-requisite or pre-requisite to participation in an innocence program. Does your school have such a class? If so, taking it would be great preparation. Most law schools require criminal procedure but if yours does not, take it anyway. If your school does not require substantive criminal law, this is also highly recommended. Some schools also offer classes on interviewing. Taking a full course on interviewing will benefit you no matter what

[8] I promised honesty. Actually, he wants to be a stand-up comic and I want him to be in an innocence program. No, he already is a stand-up comic. Only the parents reading this footnote will understand this. He really does do my power-points though.

sort of law you practice post-graduation, and you will find yourself a step ahead in any field. Very few students or new lawyers[9] interview very well.

Here are other sources of information to better inform you about innocence programs. Many of these activities some innocence programs will be doing during the program anyway. I am not suggesting that the below list is necessary as a prerequisite for innocence work and certainly the whole list is unnecessary. However, those who are interested in learning more about innocence work can do one or more of the following:

1) Talk to others who have taken the program you are interested in.
2) Visit a jail.
3) Ask if the program needs volunteers.
4) Take a trial skills class.
5) Take a legal writing course if one is not required (and do well in the course).
6) Read *Actual Innocence: When Justice Goes Wrong and How to Make it Right,* Barry Scheck, Peter Neufield, and Jim Dwyer.
7) Watch Showtime Documentary *After Innocence.*
8) Watch Movie *Conviction*, starring Hilary Swank and Sam Rockwell.
9) Watch Frontline: *Death by Fire.*
10) Watch Frontline: *The Confessions.*
11) Read *Wrongful Convictions: Cases and Materials* by Justin Brooks.
12) Finish reading this book (needless to say!).

As you can see, popcorn is a staple for innocence work (and don't forget the coffee!).

[9] I said this book was honest: very few lawyers, new or experienced, are highly skilled at interviewing.

Chapter Five

How to Survive an Innocence Program and Other Life Threatening Situations[10]

The twenty questions in Chapter Three illustrate how working with innocent prisoners is unlike any experience you have ever had. However, if you follow the advice in this book, an innocence program need not be threatening in any way.

Some students get attached to their clients. This is normal and expected. It shows commitment and humanity. Unlike other criminal clinics or the criminal defense profession in general, you will often firmly believe that your client is innocent. Accordingly, a common coping mechanism that many public defenders use after losing a case, i.e. reminding themselves that the client is responsible for the consequences of his actions, is unavailable to you. Further, the laws in many states make it tremendously hard to make meaningful progress on post-conviction cases. Dealing with hurdles in the law when you strongly believe that your client is innocent is difficult.

What should you do when a client with a compelling case of innocence is at a dead end? Should you reject that innocent client, knowing that your program is the prisoner's last resort? Or should you keep looking; not giving up until something gets the client in the door and into court? If you keep looking, what happens to the mounds of clients' letters waiting to be read? Is the golden ticket going to just wait in a pile until after you graduate? These questions are not for the book to answer, but they are necessary questions for you to consider before you decide what path you will travel in a particular case. These issues require consultation with your supervisor and colleagues. Discussions are immensely helpful, because these are hard questions with painful results for someone no matter which path you follow. Remember that your opinion is important and is valued by those around you, including your supervisor or director, and your peers. Teamwork and learning to work in a group or with a partner is a tremendously important skill for innocence work, any legal job, and life in general.

---

[10] By "life threatening situation" I mean situations that may change your life for the worse and lead you to be unhappy or depressed – like law school or filing for bankruptcy. In an innocence program your clients are in the life threatening situation but you may experience some of their struggle.

Problems with your cases may keep you up at night. It is healthy and even motivating to allow yourself to worry about a client or to be concerned with issues in the case. However, do not allow the anxiety to consume you. Remember that you did not cause the societal problems that led to innocent people being incarcerated and that you are carrying the hefty load of attempting to right these wrongs. If you are told that a case is over and that you have lost when you still feel the client is innocent, don't give up right away – keep thinking – keep talking – keep asking. Ask your supervisor about any crazy idea you can come up with. It can't hurt. As the title suggests, don't be afraid to ask – this is a person's life.

You will not always succeed but you must always try your best – and keep trying when someone's life is in your hands. However, trying your best does not mean devoting your life to the cause. In order to do true good in the world, you must take care of yourself first. You must have a happy life of your own and you must be careful not to burn yourself out. This is like the crashing airplane rule: put your own air mask on before attempting to help others with their air masks. Sadly, many of your cases will be like a crashing airplane and if you don't put your air mask on, you might not be able to breathe. If you cannot breathe, you certainly cannot help your clients.[11] So put your air mask on! Here is how. Follow these rules no matter how busy your professors, friends, or family try to make you:

1) Never give up things that make you happy – be it a hobby, a yearly trip or any activity.
2) Always eat well and get enough rest.
3) Make time for friends, family, relationships.
4) Make time for simple fun.
5) Do not ever feel guilty about 1) through 4). Aunt Petunia can wait and have Sunday morning brunch with you another time – you can sleep until noon once in a while.

At this moment, any of you who are in law school are either laughing at how ridiculous these five suggestions are because the day is 24 hours long and not 36 hours long, or you are setting the book on fire. Before you light the match, read a little further. You will not fail out of school if you take this advice. Rather, you might have a much happier and successful life in the long run. I have two activities for you to do in order to illustrate this (Yes, you do have time for these

[11] Here is another law school analogy. Law school is a crashing airplane and you will suffocate without the air mask. The exit rows are a bit more difficult to locate at law schools.

two activities). First, list three personal qualities you had before law school, then three qualities you have (or had) during law school, then list three qualities you want to have when you are at your prime (mid-forties about forty four and four months old – a particularly nice age I might add). Stop reading, go write them down and then come back. If you are not in law school, use the analogous activity in your life (e.g. if you are in journalism school use that). I am not positive that this exercise works for folks other than those wounded by law schools. However, I feel certain other graduate schools have their own special ways of causing student hardship.

Finished? The first three adjectives listed by most students are very positive ("hopeful", "ambitious", "fun"), the law school adjectives are terrible ("miserable", "worried", "sleep deprived"), and the last three adjectives are even better than the first three ("rich", "happy", "generous"). Not many of us would dispute that real world lawyering is harder than law school.[12] (If you do dispute this, please get out more.) Moreover, after working as a full-time lawyer for a few years, you might also have a family, a mortgage, and work pressures you have never known before. So how will all of you improve so dramatically under even worse conditions than law school? This book regrets to be the bearer of bad news but unless you change something soon, the way you describe yourself now in law school will only deteriorate as life gets harder. Hence the origination of a number of lawyer jokes. For example *"How do you save a lawyer from drowning?"* [13] See the footnote for the answer. Lawyers, as a profession, get burned out, turn to drugs, get depressed, commit suicide and get divorced with much greater frequency than other professions[14]. This includes dentists and postal workers. If you consider the issues involved now and follow the five rules above, none of this need be your fate.

Activity number two: imagine that you are at your own funeral[15] and write your own eulogy.[16] This activity assumes you lived a long life and died at an old age. What would you want the speaker to say? Then think hard about whether you are living your life in a way that will lead to those things being said about you. We have all heard the saying, "*Nobody says 'I wish I had billed more hours' on their*

---

[12] Maybe you don't know this. Trust me – it is.

[13] Shoot him before he hits the water.

[14] Patrick J. Schiltz, *On Being a Happy, Health, and Ethical Member of an Unhappy, Unhealthy, and Unethical Profession,* 52 Vand. L. Rev. 871 (1999).

[15] I know this is morbid. If you must, imagine your retirement dinner and write a retirement speech that someone else gives for you.

[16] I mean actually do this. Go!

death bed." In other words, do what you can, take your obligations seriously but also take the quality of your life seriously. Having given this exercise to hundreds of students over the years, students regularly wish for a life that is filled with wealth, ample family time, success at work, a stellar professional reputation, travels around the world, and a perfect, adoring (usually quite large) family. Most of you will also describe some unheard of achievement like becoming the youngest partner ever of the best law firm around or the first president to attain world peace. Although all of you do this seriously, with every expectation that all of this can be achieved, sadly, you have likely given no thought to questions like "When will there be a day where I can spend time with my gorgeous twins and also bill 10 hours?" Or, "When will I have time to take that trip to Venice with my family of five if I expect to be the youngest partner ever?" You may be able to have all of these things and more, but only if you think ahead about what your true desires are and plan how you will achieve them. You can have most things you truly want in life, just not at the same time. You must make choices and prioritize. If family is your top priority, then becoming a partner rather than becoming the youngest partner ever may make you a very happy person, and that achievement may come later in your life if you wish to spend time with your family.

All of this therapy talk illustrates the point that your work in an innocence program must be reflective. In other words, as you speak to incarcerated clients seeking your help or thanking you, you must consider what this means to you. Does this matter to you in the long term or does it just make you smile temporarily? Work in the area of the public's interest rarely lands you a job in a big firm, but it may help you find yourself working with individuals who could not otherwise afford legal assistance. Ask yourself how important it is to you that those less fortunate receive the same high quality representation as the client paying $550 per hour. Think about the meaning of your work for the innocence cause and what it means to you and how it makes you feel. If it makes you feel happy but broke and busy, how does that fit into your future plans? Will you still be content if your family vacations are at the Pop Century Budget Resort in Disney World instead of at the Ritz Carlton in London? What if vacations are few and far between? As stated at the outset, there is no shame in saying "This is not for me".

So far this chapter has focused on your ability to cope with feelings of helplessness or fatigue, emotions you may experience when advocating for an innocent client. Inherently, innocence programs also deal with gruesome crimes, and dead or traumatized victims.[17] Your client is usually traumatized as well. More

[17] Or traumatized *and* dead.

often than not, the crimes you confront in your cases will be atrocious. Innocence programs tend to handle the most serious types of cases with the stiffest penalties. In short, everyone is traumatized and suffering. You will need to examine crime scene photos and yes, this includes the medical examiner's photos of the heart in a metal bowl, the victim's chest splayed open and the blood, lots and lots of blood – it's better than any zombie movie. This is real, and enough to gag any tough guy.

Criminal lawyers, indeed all lawyers, deal in suffering, and must find ways to cope. It is particularly distressing when the cases involve child victims, and many do. Is the answer to detach yourself from the pain? If you detach yourself from the suffering of the victims and your client, can you avoid any secondary trauma? Perhaps. I suggest to you, however, that unless you embrace the pain of the entire cast of characters in your case, you cannot properly investigate or litigate the case. What do I mean by embrace? I mean recognize it, understand it, and reflect upon it. Never ignore it. The pain is an integral part of any homicide, rape or violent crime.

There are things you can do so that you are not traumatized. For example, carve out a time for yourself where you put the cases away. Imagine a cardboard box and visualize that all of your cases and all of the problems associated with the cases, together with everyone's pain and suffering, are inside that box. Then imagine putting the lid on that box and a tight bungee cord around it. Tell yourself that you will not open the box until you are ready to deal with its contents again. This mental exercise can be done with a treasure chest and a key as well, etc. Whatever suits you and helps you put away your stress for some relaxation time.

It is also important for you to have someone to talk to. Keep the rules of confidentiality in mind (See *The Innocence Network Guide to Ethics and Best Practices*). To avoid confidentiality issues you could talk to another student in the program, or the director, or use a free form writing journal. Do not hold in all of your stress and worries until you explode, this is not only bad for you but bad for anyone standing in your near vicinity. Hold it in when you have to, then lock your door and cry. This goes for you men too. If you are in court and the judge is yelling at you and telling you that you are incompetent, that is not the time to cry, yell, or give up. When court convenes feel free to go home or go to your office and cry until you have the world's biggest headache or sleep for days and then try to figure out if you really did anything wrong or the judge is just off base.

The mind naturally uses defense mechanisms to protect itself – this is healthy and often necessary when dealing with traumatic issues. The balance between the need to understand the emotional and painful issues involved in a case and the need to protect oneself from trauma and maintain the ability to make rational and thoughtful judgments is difficult and comes with experience. While the suffering must be recognized and reflected upon, at the same time, it is healthy for lawyers or students to distance themselves somewhat from the actual horrifying events that occurred to the victims or innocent inmate, otherwise they would be unable to adequately defend their clients. Conversely, it is also often necessary for the student or attorney to place themselves in the mind of the victim in order to investigate the case. The method that will allow you to distance yourself from those individuals in your case who have suffered, yet simultaneously see the world through their eyes, is to convince yourself that these things could never happen to you. This is done by reminding yourself of all the ways in which the person who suffered trauma acted in ways that you would never act, or lived a life you will never live. Of course, we all know any of these nightmares could come true for any of us at any time. Yet, if we admitted this to ourselves, we could not do our jobs fully and properly without suffering unduly. Luckily, our brains do much of this distancing for us unconsciously. This is not the only way to avoid feelings of stress and trauma. Humor is a remarkable healer of stress.

As the comic George Carlin once said ***"Laugh often, long and loud. Laugh until you gasp for breath."*** One of the best ways to deal with emotional trauma is to laugh. Laughter leads to catharsis and catharsis leads to healing. Shared humor, sometimes referred to as "gallows humor," is often a very constructive way to suppress the distressing, helpless feelings that are inevitable when working with traumatic situations. Studies show that humor, a natural defense mechanism, is an effective tool in distancing oneself from trauma and reducing stress. In short, it is sometimes okay to make a joke or two about your cases; it helps. Yes, even the horrible cases. There are, however, parameters about joking about others' pain and suffering.

1) Never joke about cases around anyone who is connected to the case other than in the program.
2) Avoid vulgar and foul language.
3) Before making a joke or immediately after, – provide disclaimers along the lines of *"you just gotta joke about this stuff sometimes to get through."* Do this until you are sure those around you are not offended by mild humor regarding the cases.
4) Do not joke in front of your professor or supervisor unless you have obtained specific permission or your professor does it too and encourages you to laugh a bit as well.

5) Use good, mature judgment and do not take joking too far or do it too often – always remember you are dealing with someone's very serious pain and suffering.
6) Be sensitive about making jokes around classmates and colleagues – some of them may have been victims of crimes or know victims of serious crimes, and the jokes could be hurtful to them (e.g. rape).

If you do find that it takes the load off a bit, experiment with it and smile. Many innocence program students reported that a clinic class setting where jokes could be made in safety contributed to an atmosphere of camaraderie and played a major role in helping them handle the horrific issues they dealt with day in and day out.[18] It helped the students sort out what issues were big issues and worthy of worry and which issues were not worth sweating over.

"Don't sweat the petty things and don't pet the sweaty things"
George Carlin

It is easy to get overwhelmed in an innocence program. Getting overly concerned over small matters is easy to do when you are overwhelmed. To help reduce the occurrence of this common issue, you must prioritize and organize. I implore you to invest in whatever type of organizational system works best for you. Your time will be tight and you will often not get everything done on the first try. It is therefore important that you have clearly delineated what must get done and what can wait. If you are the type of person who worries over everything or can't tolerate not getting everything done, try some of the remedies above: laugh, close the box on your cases, and participate in activities that are important to your personal life. Even if you decide that public interest work or innocence work is not for you now or post-graduation, you still need to get through law school[19]. The suggestions from this chapter will reduce your stress, likely raise your grades, and could even reduce your caffeine intake – although I would not bet on that last one.[20]

---

[18] Miami Law Innocence Clinic, 2011 and 2012.
[19] Recall law school itself is an identified life threatening situation.
[20] For those reading this book who notice I poke fun at law schools, I want to clarify that I adore my students and my job at a fine law school. I am concerned, however, for those students who we see day after day (mostly in the library), whose facial twitching keeps getting worse and worse, and each day they are a shade paler. Are they ok?

PART II
PROCESS AND PROCEDURES OF INNOCENCE PROGRAMS

Chapter Six

General Innocence Program Procedures and Ethical Concerns

As mentioned earlier, innocence programs are structured in many different ways. Law schools are not the only type of school to run these programs. For example, a few journalism schools are involved with innocence programs and seek exonerations through the media. These programs are very successful and are a valuable component of the innocence movement. Like law school students in innocence programs, journalism students should find this book useful (and they might sigh in relief that they did not go to law school). Although the structure of innocence programs varies, an overview of the most common procedures is useful for understanding the basics of an innocence program. The following is a step-by-step process that describes what an innocence program typically does when it receives a letter from an inmate. Again, please be aware that programs differ in their structure and what follows is just an example of the best practices for an innocence program.

1) The program receives a letter from the inmate.
2) The letter is documented (usually in a software program). After it is documented, the letter may wait for a short time until staff is available to review it. However, it is important that the initial letter from the inmate is reviewed quickly in order to insure that any deadlines are not missed. There should be very little, if any, backlog here.
3) Either a paralegal, an intake coordinator, a student or another staff member reads the letter and screens it to see if it meets the program's screening criteria.
4) Unless the letter obviously does not meet the program's criteria, an application is sent to the inmate along with a letter asking him to complete the application and return it to the program.
5) Documentation of the request is made.

6) If the letter is clear that the inmate's case does not meet the program's screening criteria (e.g. "I killed him but the judge should not have given me so long in prison. Please help"), a denial letter is sent.
7) Documentation of the reasons for the denial is then made.
8) When an application is received, it is also documented and again may wait until staff is available to review. This is the point where the inmate may wait longer and a backlog may exist for some time.
9) A letter confirming receipt of the application is sent to the client. This letter also informs the client that he may be on a waiting list and that the program will review his case as soon as possible. This letter also informs the client that the waiting time does not imply that the program has accepted his case or created the attorney-client relationship.
10) A student, attorney, or other designated staff member reviews the application carefully to ascertain if the client meets the program's screening criteria.
11) If the client does not meet the screening criteria, a denial letter is sent and documented.
12) If the criteria are met, then the case moves into the investigation stage and this is documented.
13) If, after a complete investigation, a decision is made that there is no viable claim to actual innocence, a denial letter is sent, family is spoken to and the client is called. All of this is documented. A denial at this stage requires detailed written documentation of the investigation done and the reasons for the denial. See an example of a denial request form in the appendix.
14) A memorandum is written regarding the reasons for the denial and all steps taken to investigate.
15) If, after a complete investigation, a decision is made that the client does have a viable claim to actual innocence, then the proper avenue for a motion for post-conviction relief is discussed and determined with the supervisor.
16) At this point, a retainer agreement is signed and the program may file a notice of appearance.[21] Programs are encouraged to have a retainer signed as early in the case as is practical.[22]

---

[21] Programs differ widely on when they will file a notice of appearance. This decision will be up to your director or supervisor. It falls under the category of "ask questions!"

[22] Programs differ on when it is appropriate to sign a retainer.

17) Are you getting the picture that every single thing is documented?
18) Students or designated staff members investigate the case thoroughly.
19) Everything done is documented – including unanswered phone calls.
20) If you are working in a team – the investigation is done together and decisions made together.
21) In most programs, students may not call witnesses, send letters or make decisions on cases without authorization and discussion with their supervisor.
22) In most programs that are run in an academic setting, supervisors guide the students as opposed to simply telling the students what to do. Students learn how to work up and investigate cases independently (with their supervisor's oversight).
23) In many programs you may write the motion.
24) In some programs, if you are certified and obtain a hearing, you might argue the motion.
25) If you are completing a semester and not returning to the program, graduating, or not returning to the innocence program for any reason, it is critical that, before you leave, you write a summary memo on any case that is still open so that the incoming student will be thoroughly informed as to the status of the case.

The above list of steps assumes that everything went as planned. You know what they say about assuming? Well, just don't do it. Cases, especially real cases with real human beings, do not generally go as planned. Take the above steps as merely a guide as to what should happen.[23] Further, programs differ in procedures and your program may do things a bit differently. However, certainly in any program most of the above list will need to be done in some fashion. You must learn the procedure of your own program and proceed in the manner that your director instructs. Remember who is boss.[24]

One of the first things you will likely do in an innocence program is sign a confidentiality agreement. A sample can be found in the appendix. This is one of the most important documents in an innocence program. Although you are not a lawyer yet, you will come in contact with many confidential documents and have many confidential communications. Recall that your work in an innocence

[23] Again, these 25 steps are only an example. Different programs may have different steps.
[24] Not this book.

program affects the lives of real people unlike many other classes you may have taken in school. You may acquire a duty to maintain the confidentiality of client communications. It is incumbent on you to learn the rules of ethics that apply to your role in the innocence program. This will depend on your duties in the program. The best place to look is "*The Innocence Network: Guide to Ethics and Best Practices for Innocence Practioners*"[25] and "*Ethical Issue for Innocence Projects: An Initial Primer* by Ellen Suni[26]. Ethical issues in an innocence program can be complicated and extensive and this book can only touch the surface. If you have any questions regarding any ethical concerns please consult your supervisors.

You might think facts that you obtain from court files are not confidential, but this is not necessarily true. Model Rule of Professional Conduct 1.6 provides that confidentiality applies to any "information relating to the representation of a client" without an explicit public records exception. Thus, this question hinges on whether the attorney-client relationship has formed and whether the program is representing the client. In any event, it is your obligation to function in the best interest of your client. This usually involves not speaking about your clients' cases to anyone outside of the program, whether confidential or not, unless you are investigating the case. Many times, of course, you will need to speak to third parties during your investigation of a case to gather information. It may be best to obtain your client's consent for you to do this at the outset of your investigation, even before any attorney-client relationship has developed. Many application forms, once signed by the client, provide the innocence program consent to speak to whomever necessary and conduct an investigation. This makes it unnecessary to contact the client each time the program wishes to move forward with any investigation.

The duty of confidentiality often develops well before an attorney-client relationship. Pursuant to Model Rule of Professional Conduct 1.6, the activities a program must undertake to screen and investigate a case inherently create a duty of confidentiality. You must always be aware of this and act accordingly. The rules of confidentiality can be very complicated, and cannot be fully explained here. Discuss these rules of ethics with your supervisor. In general, the duty of confidentiality prohibits a program from disclosing client information or using that

---

[25] You can obtain this document through the Google search engine or you can find it on the innocence project's website.

[26] This is available through SSRN at http://papers.ssrn.com/sol3/papers.cfm?abstract_id=1016823.

information to the disadvantage of the client. A program still owes a duty of confidentiality to the prospective client even when an attorney-client relationship has not been formed. Virtually all information gleaned during the screening or initial investigatory phase is likely to fall within the ambit of the duty of confidentiality.[27] The program must often contact third parties to gather information about a case, so a written release must be obtained from the prospective client granting informed consent to share otherwise confidential information to investigate the case. As noted above, many applications include such informed consent as part of the application. Note that communications with police officers and prosecutors are not considered confidential.

Programs differ as to when the attorney–client relationship begins between the inmate and the program. Some designate it as the time the program begins to investigate the case and others consider it to attach when pleadings are filed. It is your obligation to find out your program's policy on this matter. It is important to establish precisely when the attorney-client relationship is formed. The existence of an attorney-client relationship carries professional obligations. Once created, lawyers are obligated to abide by their fiduciary[28] duty to the client. As a general matter, the attorney-client relationship is formed when a prospective client communicates the intent to seek legal services and the program communicates consent to provide those services. Alternately, the attorney-client relationship may form when the program fails to communicate the lack of consent to provide services despite the fact that they reasonably should know that the prospective client is reasonably relying on the program to provide legal services.

When a program is extensively researching or investigating a case but has not filed pleadings, the inmate may make a natural assumption that the attorney-client relationship is formed and that relationship carries obligations. It is important that

---

[27] *See* Model Rule 1.6 in *The Innocence Network: Guide to Ethics & Best Practices for Innocence Project Practitioners.*

[28] A fiduciary relationship is a relationship of trust. There does not have to be money involved as is commonly misunderstood. Sorry, innocence work brings good feelings and no money. However it could mean money for your client; innocence programs should develop policies and procedures for retaining or referring clients to lawyers for potential compensation claims and other legal matters. The policies should be reviewed with outside counsel to ensure that ethical obligations are met and that the non-profit status of the program, if applicable, is adequately protected.

when you speak to the client you inform him of the exact status of the attorney-client relationship and whether it has been formed. This includes any time you have communication with your client by letter or email. The attorney-client relationship can form long before you have accepted the inmate as a client so you must keep the individual informed as to the limitations of your assistance at all times. Further, cases that are in a program's backlog may end up forming an attorney-client relationship because the inmate assumes that his or her case has been accepted into the program due to the extensive period of time his or her case has been held by the program. It would be prudent to advise these waiting clients that they can expect to wait a period of time and such waiting does not form an attorney-client relationship.

Even once you have agreed to represent a client there will be limitations to your representation and you must make that explicit in your retainer agreement and continually remind your client of these limitations. Every innocence program must have a clear retainer agreement. The retainer should be signed as soon as the attorney-client relationship is formed. The agreement should make clear the scope and limitations of the program's representation. An innocence program must consult and obtain informed consent from clients with regard to the means by which the program can seek to accomplish his goals. Clients should be kept up to date and informed about the status of their cases. Any of the client's requests for information should be complied with reasonably and promptly. The attorney or student should explain matters to the extent necessary to allow the client to make informed decisions about his representation. It is very important to maintain regular contact and provide updates to a client after having initial contact with him.

Be on the lookout for conflicts of interest. Every innocence program must make a diligent effort to identify, guard against, and respond to potential and actual conflicts of interest. This duty of loyalty is only required once an attorney-client relationship has been established (usually when active representation has commenced), not to cases in the screening and investigation stages. A reasonable duty of care is still owed to potential clients during the screening process. The program should not represent a client when there is a concurrent conflict of interest. A concurrent conflict of interest exists when (1) representation of one client adversely affects the program's ability to represent another current client, or (2) the representation of one client will be limited by the program's responsibilities to another client (current or former), to a third party, or to the personal interests of the attorney and students assigned to the case. This applies to both program clients and clients program participants represent outside of the innocence program.[29]

A program must inform the client that law (or other type) students will be working on his or her case, what the role of the students is, and that the students are being supervised by an attorney. Students may screen and investigate cases. Students may be responsible for updating and maintaining client files during the investigative process. Students may also participate in legal writing assignments, client communications, and some stages of litigation under the supervision of an attorney. It is recommended that all students participate in training at the beginning of each semester of enrollment to ensure that they will consistently follow the program's procedures. It is also recommended that clients be advised how fortunate they are to have you on their case.

When you are investigating and interviewing a potential witness there are rules to remember. When conducting a witness or client interview, the innocence program member must disclose who he or she is, who he or she works for, and on whose behalf he or she is appearing. However, the program does not necessarily speak to witnesses on the behalf of the client when the case is in the screening or investigation stage because no formal attorney-client relationship has been formed. The program members cannot provide a witness with legal advice because that would likely create a conflict of interest. Further, if the member conducting the interview is a student, providing legal advice would constitute unauthorized practice of law. Student communications with clients should be conducted under the supervision of an attorney whenever possible. Interviewing will be discussed further in Chapter Ten.

Most programs will have clearly delineated responsibilities and expectations for you. Regardless of the form in which those responsibilities are communicated to you, you must be sure to understand and follow them. If you do not understand something about your responsibilities, you must ask your director or supervisor, preferably in front of any other students also in the program. This is because I can almost guarantee that some of the students will think to themselves "Whew, am I glad he asked that question, I was clueless...."

Finally, each innocence program should establish an organized case management system for logging status updates and tracking the progress of cases. Clearly defined stages of investigation and representation should mark each case

---

[29] *Id.*

file. Students must continuously update the case files for their assigned cases with information about the actions they took and memorandum regarding any communications and research performed. Many programs require reports to be filed on a weekly basis. It is also common to utilize an electronic filing system that consolidates the case notes, updates, and file documents in one convenient place. It works well to view your innocence program as though it were a law firm and as though you were an associate in the firm and your supervisors are the partners. The Innocence Network requires each member innocence program to submit a summary of case-tracking information in an Annual Network Report. This report should include the number of solicitations for assistance received, the number that moved beyond the screening stages, and the number of cases at each of the identified stages of investigation and/or representation. It is essential to remain organized and to prioritize. One of the first things you may do when you receive a case is to "screen" the case.

Chapter Seven

What are Screening Criteria and How do I Screen a Case?

What follows is an outline of common screening criteria, why they are important, and what to look for when screening a letter or application from an inmate[30]. Innocence programs use a wide range of screening criteria and questions on their applications. The following is an example of the typical screening criteria used while reviewing an application to determine its suitability for further investigation. This screening example covers DNA and non-DNA cases. A sample of a typical application is in the appendix.

Step 1: Does the case meet the criteria for the program?

a) Is the inmate claiming "actual innocence"?

Actual innocence means that the client is asserting that he was not involved in the charged crime whatsoever. The client must be asserting that he is in fact innocent as opposed to claiming he should have been found not guilty at trial for other reasons (e.g. ineffective assistance of counsel).[31] Most often the client will be claiming a case of misidentification.

Think of "actual innocence" as innocent vs. not-guilty. A person may have committed the crime and be found not guilty for many fair and legal reasons. For example, if a woman is attacked by a man with a knife and he is about to kill her and she shoots him with a gun, then she still killed a man. Nonetheless, our law says that she was justified in doing so because she had to kill him to save her own life; she is legally not guilty. Most innocence programs do not take cases where the act was excusable or justifiable. Most innocence programs also do not take cases where the client should have been found not guilty for other reasons, e.g. the client had a drug addicted sleeping lawyer, even though such a client could have a viable cause of action.

[30] Programs differ regarding screening criteria.

[31] If the client is claiming actual innocence, the claims of ineffective assistance of counsel, etc. may also be raised under certain conditions. The point being there must always be an actual innocence claim involved.

In addition, it is often hard to tell from the letter alone if the inmate is claiming actual innocence. Inmates are sometimes upset with their lawyers and speak about that in the letter. This does not mean that they are not completely innocent. The inmates could simply be angry that their lawyers could not convince the jury of their innocence. This is why an application is usually needed to be sure an innocent prisoner is not overlooked.

b) The inmate must not be claiming self-defense or consensual sexual assault.

This is related to a) above. A client should not be claiming that she was involved in the crime but was justified in some way. Note that programs have the discretion to take these cases if they feel strongly about them. Guidelines are just that – guidelines. When a program believes that an innocent person is incarcerated, it will often feel a moral obligation to move forward with the investigation even when the screening criterion has not been met. The bottom line is that if you ever feel in your heart that a client is innocent, forget every guideline, take it to your supervisor, and beg your case. Nobody wants to deny assistance to an innocent inmate.

c) Has the inmate exhausted his/her appellate remedies?

If an inmate has not exhausted her appeal process, then she is still entitled to counsel (through the public defender's office if she cannot afford counsel). In these instances, the program can be fairly comfortable denying the application because motions for post-conviction relief cannot be filed until the inmate's appeal is finalized; therefore an innocence program's hands are tied until the applicant's appeal is final.

d) Was the crime committed in (enter relevant area here)?

If the crime was not committed in your program's geographical area, your procedures are likely to instruct you to refer the inmate to the appropriate innocence program in the county or area where the crime was committed. Some programs are flexible on this criterion. If you find a case that meets all of the other criteria except it is out of the jurisdiction, it might be worth a chat with your supervisor before suggesting a referral.

e) Death or non-death cases.

This depends on the program. Some programs take both death and non-death cases, and some take only one or the other. Be aware that the post-conviction law for death cases is significantly different than for non-death cases.

f) There should be enough years left on the applicant's sentence for the program to actually help the applicant.

This is another criterion that is often flexible. The reason for this criterion is that post-conviction cases could take up to five years (or longer) to reach a resolution. If, at the outset, the client has less than ten years on his sentence, the program might only save this client two years (or less) of imprisonment when many other worthy clients who are serving life sentences and need help are backlogged. Again, it is a matter of prioritizing.

g) The inmate should not currently have counsel.

This criterion is used by almost every innocence program. There can be exceptions. If a private attorney has taken on a case pro bono and needs the assistance of an innocence program, sometimes the director may decide to jointly litigate a case with private counsel. This usually happens only with very large cases or media cases.

<u>Step 2</u>: Is the inmate eligible to file a motion for post-conviction relief?

Jurisdictions have different rules regarding a client's legal ability to file a motion for post-conviction relief. Florida is one of the strictest states, allowing only two years from when the client's appeal becomes final to file a motion for post-conviction relief. If it has been more than two years, there must be new evidence that could not have been discovered by due diligence. ***You must research and learn the law in your jurisdiction regarding the filing of post-conviction motions. This should be your first priority as a member of an innocence program.*** If your jurisdiction is similar to Florida, follow these steps:

a) Is the case within 2-years of the date that the inmate's judgment and sentence became final?

Generally, this means assessing whether or not it has been more than 2 years since the date the appeal became final.

b) If the case is within the 2-year window and also meets the program's criteria, see your supervisor.

In these cases, you may be in a big rush to evaluate the case for filing of a motion for post-conviction relief before the two-year window is over.

c) If the case is outside of the 2-year window (as most will be) proceed to STEP 3.

<u>Step 3</u>: Could there be "newly discovered evidence" sufficient to satisfy the exception to the time limits?

a) Has any new evidence come to light that was not available to the trial or appellate court?

b) If yes, could this evidence have been discovered earlier by "due diligence"?

This means that the rule will not admit evidence that could have been found at the time of trial with a fair amount of effort, regardless of whether the trial attorney looked for it.

<u>Step 4</u>: Biological Evidence / DNA testing

Each jurisdiction has different guidelines and motions for post-conviction relief based on DNA testing. Please familiarize yourself with the guidelines in your jurisdiction.

a) A positive DNA test may serve as newly discovered evidence sufficient to waive the 2 year time limit.

b) Is the crime or the facts of the case such that there MIGHT be biological evidence? For example:

i. Does the crime involve rape/sexual assault? There could be biological evidence such as semen, pubic hairs, and saliva. Is it a homicide or another violent crime? Could there be blood, fingerprints, anything at all from the body, sweat, or hair? Think creatively.

c) **If you SUSPECT the existence of biological evidence, and the case meets the criteria in STEP 1, see your supervisor.** Investigation and search for the biological evidence may begin!

Most directors of innocence programs, I will take the liberty of believing, would want you to consult with them regarding any case you felt particularly compelled about even if it did not meet the screening criteria. The mission of innocence programs is to exonerate innocent persons and if you feel an individual is innocent, you should raise the issue seriously with your director. We are not in the business of giving up or letting innocent people remain in prison. Most directors are willing to try new and creative ways to help save the innocent and so should you – so don't give up too quickly. As you may have noticed, almost all of the guidelines above are negotiable so just keep your eyes open for the golden ticket.

Chapter Eight

How did this Happen? The Number One Cause of Wrongful Convictions

Eyewitness misidentifications make up seventy percent (or more) of wrongful convictions[32]. Even when a lineup is conducted with every procedure done correctly to protect the accused, eyewitness identification is prone to misidentification. A considerable number of wrongful convictions that stem from misidentification are a product of suggestive lineups and suggestive comments made by law enforcement officers (both inadvertent and willful).[33] These imperfections, coupled with jurors' tendency to weigh eyewitness evidence heavily, contribute to many wrongful convictions.

Memory

It is not unusual to incorrectly recall the details of an event and such inability does not necessarily reflect poor memory. Studies have shown that we can even come to believe that we remember events that never actually occurred.[34] When people construct a memory, they gather fragments of what they have stored and fill in the gaps with what makes most sense to them.[35] Human beings recall events by adding these bits and pieces to their recollections based on their subjective understandings of the world. As Professors Loftus and Ketchum noted, "Truth and reality, when seen through the filters of our memories, are not objective facts but subjective, interpretive realities."[36] Because these processes are unconscious, individuals generally perceive their memories as completely accurate and their reporting of what they remember as entirely truthful, no matter how

---

[32] Richard A. Rosen, *Innocence and Death*, 82 N.C. L. REV. 61, 70 n.32 (2003).
[33] *See* Samuel R. Gross et al., *Exonerations in the United States 1989 through 2003*, 95 J. CRIM. L. & CRIMINOLOGY 523, 542 (2005).
[34] ELIZABETH LOFTUS & KATHERINE KETCHAM, WITNESS FOR THE DEFENSE: THE ACCUSED, THE EYEWITNESS, AND THE EXPERT WHO PUTS MEMORY ON TRIAL 20 (1991).
[35] *Id.*
[36] *Id.*

distorted or inaccurate these memories may be.[37] An individual's memories become distorted even in the absence of external suggestion or internal personal distress. Naturally, people tailor their telling of events to the listener and the context. Each act of telling or retelling changes the teller's memory of the event.[38] Loftus and Ketchum explain, "This is why a fish story, which grows with each telling, can eventually lead the teller to believe it."[39]

Conditions such as fear, lighting, distance from the event, surprise, and personal biases such as racial stereotypes affect memory and recollection.[40] Preconceptions, conscious or unconscious, shape our memories. In one study, participants were shown four news stories, each containing an identical photograph of the same African American man. The stories described: (1) a college professor; (2) a basketball player; (3) a non-violent crime; and (4) a violent crime. After viewing the photos and reading the stories, the participants were asked to reconstruct the photo of the man for each story by selecting from an assortment of facial features. The stories involving criminal conditions resulted in the selection of more characteristically pronounced African-American facial features. This was particularly true for the violent crime scenario.[41] Participants' preconceived notions and stereotypes affected their choices.

Human memory is indeed delicate, especially regarding victims and witnesses of crimes. Fear and traumatic events may impair the initial acquisition of the memory itself.[42] At the time of the initial encounter, the witness is often in a distressed emotional state. This emotional state impairs memory acquisition. Many victims and witnesses experience substantial shock or emotional upset because of

---

[37] *Id.*
[38] Laura Engelhardt, *The Problem with Eyewitness Testimony: Commentary on a Talk by George Fisher and Barbara Tversky*, 1 STAN. J. LEGAL STUD. 25, 27 (1999).
[39] *Id.*
[40] *Id.*
[41] *Readers' Memories Of Crime Stories Influenced By Racial Stereotypes*, SCIENCE DAILY (May 6, 2004), http://www.sciencedaily.com/releases/2004/05/040506073047.htm.
[42] *Id.* However, courts persist in erroneously believing that witnesses experiencing elevated emotional states produce more accurate recollections or perceptions. For example, in *Howard v. Bouchard*, 405 F.3d 459, 473 (6th Cir. 2005), the court found that the identification was admissible in part because the witness was in a heightened state of stress at the time of the event and presumably would better remember the perpetrator as a result.

their traumatic experiences, which continue to affect them at the time of the identification. In eyewitness identification procedures, the witness's motivation to make an identification may also be very powerful. Such witnesses may seek rapid resolution and closure, leading to hasty identifications of fillers[43] in the absence of the true perpetrator. Furthermore, their recollection is often distorted and untrustworthy because of their traumatic experiences.[44]

The presence of a weapon may also influence a witness's ability to recall the face of the perpetrator. Studies show that when a weapon is present during an event, the ability for the witness to perceive the perpetrator is impaired.[45] The witness may be focusing on the weapon, rather than the culprit, during the criminal episode. Further, in one study where the weapon was placed in a prominent location, recall was worse than when the weapon was partially hidden or off to the side.[46] Conversely, other studies indicate that the location of the weapon does not affect memory accuracy.[47] An explanation for this may be that the presence of a weapon alarms the witness and leads to a higher arousal level, which in turn impairs memory acquisition. Some studies show an absence of the "weapon effect" in non-arousing classroom or laboratory settings.[48]

A variety of other external factors may influence and impair a witness's ability to recall an event or the face of a perpetrator. For example, witnesses have difficulty identifying perpetrators cross-racially, which may relate to individual internal biases. Studies show accurate suspect identification rates are much greater under same-race conditions.[49] In addition, older adults have increased difficulty with cognitive performance and perform worse in identification procedures.

---

43 A "filler" is a known innocent person placed in a lineup.

44 *See* Tom Singer, *To Tell the Truth, Memory Isn't that Good,* 63 MONT. L. REV. 337, 360 (2002).

45 Nancy Steblay, *A Meta-analytic Review of the Weapon Focus Effect,* 16 LAW & HUM. BEHAV. 413–24 (1992).

46 Thomas H. Kramer, Robert Buckhout & Paul Eugenio, *Weapon Focus, Arousal, and Eyewitness Memory: Attention Must be Paid*, 14 LAW & HUM. BEHAV. 167–84 (1990).

47 *See* Steblay, *supra* note 45 at 414.

48 *See* Kramer et al., *supra* note 46.

49 Bruce W. Behrman & Sherri[illegible]avey, *Eyewitness Identification in Actual Criminal Cases: An Archival Analysis*, *25* LAW & HUM. BEHAV. 475–91 (2001).

Ironically, older adults who recall more details about a culprit are actually more likely to make false identifications.[50]

Lineups

Suggestive lineups often occur when one person from the lineup is immediately and apparently different from the rest. This can be tested by having someone completely unrelated to the investigation select one person out of the lineup; if the unrelated individual selects the same person as the witness, it is likely that the lineup is suggestive. However, courts may still admit a lineup, even if it is unnecessarily suggestive, when certain circumstances exist.[51] Police officers sometimes taint lineups (consciously or unconsciously) through vocal inflections, pauses, head and body motions, even the mere presence of the police officer itself may be suggestive. It is therefore imperative that lineups be conducted properly. The lineup must have at least five fillers. The fillers cannot be so apparently different that the suspect stands out from the rest. The fillers must also resemble either the suspect or the description given, there must only be one suspect in the lineup, and officers may not re-use fillers.

Confidence & Reliability

Witnesses often get confirming feedback from those conducting the lineup, giving the witness a false sense of confidence. When a witness says something and the officer confirms it, the witness's mind will actually adopt that memory as quickly and readily as the real memory. Suppose that a victim views a lineup of all men wearing baseball caps. The victim did not mention a cap of any kind in her description of the perpetrator when she was asked to describe him. Each man in the lineup is wearing a different color cap. The victim identifies the man wearing the red cap. Then the officer states: *"The man we caught with your jewelry in his pocket had a red cap on, did the man who attacked you have a red cap on?"* The victim will no doubt form a very real recollection of her attacker wearing a red cap now. This is not a real memory but one created by the police officer. Our memories change so easily because memory is fungible and malleable.[52] This confirming feedback leads to witness confidence. An individual's own biases and personal history also create false memories, almost

---

[50] *Id.*

[51] *See* Neil v. Biggers, 409 U.S. 188, 197 (1972).

[52] Gary L. Wells, *Eyewitness Identification: Systemic Reforms*, 2006 WIS. L. REV. 615, 621 (2006).

like a puzzle with pieces missing that witnesses fill in using their own experiences, biases, and information around them.

One possible method of documenting this false sense of confidence is for the police officers to write down the witness's level of confidence prior to anything being said about the identification. This helps the defense attorney show the rise in the witness's confidence from the identification to trial to expose the false identification. There is no true correlation between confidence and accuracy of the identification. The most effective protection against suggestion in a lineup is double blind testing where the police officer does not know who the suspect is and therefore cannot even subconsciously be suggestive. Double blind testing avoids confidence inflation, unintentional cuing to the witness, and confirming feedback.

Courts admit suggestive identification procedures if they are "reliable". This type of reliability is measured using the factors from *Neil v. Biggers*[53]. In *Neil v. Biggers* the United States Supreme Court asserted that reliability is the linchpin of the whole process.[54] Couldn't they have found a better word than "linchpin"? How about "sine qua non"? Even that is better than "linchpin". Who uses the word "linchpin"? *"Sure, I'd love to do dinner with you guys next Saturday but the linchpin of the deal is that I have to finish my Contracts homework before then."* I digress, back to work. When a lineup has been found to be suggestive, courts have admitted the identification if they have found it to be reliable. "Reliable" is assessed by indicia of reliability that is meant to indicate the guilty party has been identified. *Biggers* looks at five reliability factors to determine whether the witness identified the proper person:[55]

1. Degree of attention.
2. Opportunity of witness to view criminal at time of crime.
3. Accuracy of witness' prior description of the criminal.
4. Level of certainty demonstrated by witness at confrontation.
5. Time between the crime and the identification (time-incident).

Although the *Biggers* factors appear to test the correctness of an identification, in fact, they do not. All of the *Biggers* factors are influenced by suggestiveness and the types of feedback that can artificially inflate confidence. This is because the majority of the *Biggers* factors rely on self-reports of the witness. If the police

---

[53] *See Neil,* 409 U.S. 188 at 199.
[54] *See Id.*
[55] *Id.*

officer suggested to the witness that suspect number three stole her purse, the witness is likely to identify number three even if at first she was unsure. After she identifies number three, if the officer says "Good job! We found your wallet in his car" (confirming feedback), the victim will feel very sure that number three did the crime. Now the high level of the victim's confidence will lead her to report to the Court that she is very certain that he is culprit, that she got a great view of him, and she was paying very close attention (all *Biggers* factors). Had the police officer not provided the suggestion to boost the victim from unsure to very confident, she would have failed the *Biggers* factors or perhaps not made an identification at all. What results is that impermissible suggestion in identification procedures leads to apparently increased reliability via the *Biggers* factors test for reliability.

The number one solution for suggestive identification procedures would be for police to follow a set of prophylactic guidelines to protect against wrongful convictions. The most important of these guidelines would be to administer double blind lineups. A double blind lineup is one where the administrator does not know who the suspect is and therefore cannot make willful or inadvertent comments or give clues to the witness as to who the suspect is in the lineup. A complete list of recommended guidelines can be found at the Innocence Project website[56].

---

[56] http://www.innocenceproject.org/understand/Eyewitness-Misidentification.php and click on *learn about reform.*

Chapter Nine

Other Causes of Wrongful Convictions

This section briefly reviews some common causes of wrongful convictions. The causes are so numerous that it could take an entire semester to scratch the surface. The ones noted in this book, however, serve as a reminder of some the issues that you should be looking for when you investigate your cases. The case law in each area is extensive. This section is a short primer; if you were going for a run (which in a sense you are), this section would merely tell you where to find your running shoes.

False Confessions

Those unfamiliar with false confessions often think false confessions are uncommon or unlikely. Not so. Under the right conditions, I could get you to say that this is the most interesting book you have ever read. False confessions are dangerous because jurors love confessions and most believe that false confessions do not happen. Although many individuals who give false confessions are mentally disabled or under the influence of alcohol/drugs, a false confession can come from sober individuals at any intelligence level. The particular interrogations that elicit false confessions are often lengthy, stressful and strenuous and can cause innocent people to confess to crimes they did not commit. For instance, the average interrogation lasts about two hours while false confession interrogations average 36 – 48 hours[57].

There are three types of false confessions: voluntary, compliant, and internalized. Voluntary confessions occur when a suspect lies about a crime for fame or attention. Compliant confessions occur when the suspect capitulates to escape punishment, obtain a reward, or just gets scared. Internalized confessions happen when the suspect is tricked into believing that he or she actually committed the crime. Such confessions occur largely as a result of an officer's use of false

[57] Saul M. Kassin, *On the Psychology of Confessions: Does Innocence Put Innocents at Risk?* , AMERICAN PSYCHOLOGIST, Apr. 2005, at 217.

evidence (which is permitted by law) and the employment of the Reid Technique[58] during the interrogation. The Reid Technique has essentially three components:

1. *Isolation*: often in a special interrogation room, this increases anxiety and the incentive to escape
2. *Confrontation*: in which the suspect is accused of the crime, presented with evidence, real or manufactured, and blocked from denial;
3. *Minimization*: in which the crime is morally justified by a sympathetic interrogator, leading suspects to see confession as a possible means of "escape", the officers present the suspect with a "moral way out."

This technique works largely because of the social impact theory, which is similar to peer pressure and causes suspects to cooperate or confess regardless of the truth. The social impact theory generally consists of the following:

1. *Power*: police exert power over the suspect by simply being police, using their authority or by being threatening.
2. *Numbers*: several police interrogate the suspect.
3. *Proximity*: the suspect is required to remain is a small room with several officers who intentionally encroach on his personal space and "get in his face."

The police asking the questions already presume that the suspect is guilty. This causes them to ask guilt presumptive questions in the interrogation, which makes the innocent suspect sound increasingly anxious and defensive. The isolation aspect increases anxiety and the suspect's desire to escape. These conditions create a self-fulfilling prophecy. Because the police assume the suspect is lying, they look for signs to confirm those assumptions. Actions that are common when a person is anxious or nervous are interpreted by the police as signs of guilt.

Police officers may also receive deception detection training. This causes them to feel an elevated sense of self-assurance in their ability to detect lies. Studies show that in high stakes lies, police with training may be marginally better than an ordinary civilian at detecting a lie; however, in all other situations, they are no better than anyone else. Further, although police are no more talented than others

---

[58] FRED E. INBAU, JOHN E. REID, JOSEPH O. BUCKLEY & BRIAN C. JAYNE, CRIMINAL INTERROGATIONS AND CONFESSIONS XI-XII (4th ed. 2004).

in assessing if someone is lying, they are usually far more confident in their assessments; this false sense of confidence becomes dangerous.[59]

Innocence puts innocent suspects at risk for several reasons. First, innocent individuals are often steadfast and relentless in professing their innocence. This leads to highly confrontational interrogations because the harder the suspect pushes his innocence, the harder the police officer pushes in the other direction. This makes the innocent person appear guilty by his body language and increasingly frantic or aggressive mannerisms. Second, innocent people tend to waive their Miranda rights because they feel that they have nothing to hide and invoking their rights may make them look guilty. Thus, innocent suspects may spend more time in the interrogation room than guilty suspects. Third, innocent people tend to willingly agree to be included in lineups falsely believing that there is no way that they would be selected. Yet, if she is placed in a lineup the police already assumes she is guilty and are likely to suggest her selection to the witness. Fourth, innocent people suffer from the illusion of transparency. In other words, those who know they are innocent are more likely to willingly engage with the police officer because they believe their innocence will shine through in their interactions.[60] The illusion of transparency leads the innocent suspect to believe a confession will allow him to escape the current uncomfortable situation and his innocence will be obvious to everyone once he gets out of there and can explain.

Confessions taint other evidence in a case as well. For example, in one study[61] 60% of the witnesses who had identified a subject in the original lineup changed their mind because they were told there was a confession in the case and it was not the person they had identified. Additionally, in that same study, 44% of the witnesses who initially did not identify anyone in the lineup, changed their mind and identified a suspect after also being told that someone in the lineup confessed. When questioned afterwards, these witnesses said they believed the police; when the police said someone confessed, they were convinced that the person who confessed had to be guilty, and they felt an obligation to identify someone. Half the time, they thought that the new information had merely refreshed their memories and they were now actually remembering the correct subject. Even alibi witnesses sometimes change their stories. In some cases where

---

[59] Kassin, *supra* note 57 at 217.

[60] *See Id.*

[61] Lisa E. Hasel & Saul M. Kassin, *On the Presumption of Evidentiary Independence: Can Confessions Corrupt Eyewitness Identifications?*, ASSOCIATION FOR PSYCHOLOGICAL SCIENCE, Jan. 1, 2009.

a crime occurs, there are alibi witnesses for the suspect. When these witnesses are told that the suspect confessed, they suddenly begin to question their own memories. They begin to remember things that would complete the puzzle with the false confession. Often the alibi witnesses recant their alibi and withdraw their initial statement after learning of a confession.

Ineffective Assistance of Counsel

The rule to determine if an attorney's assistance was ineffective comes from *Strickland v. Washington*[62]. The defendant must first prove that the attorney's advice was deficient using an objective standard of reasonableness. Then the defendant must show that the deficient performance prejudiced the defense. This is subjective and speculative because it is impossible to know what would have happened had the attorney not made the claimed mistakes. The defendant has to show that the lawyer was making errors that were so serious that the lawyer was not acting as counsel.[63] Further, if a court finds that a lawyer's conduct was trial strategy, it will usually not be considered ineffective unless the court finds that the trial strategy was unreasonable, which is quite rare. In *Wiggins v. Smith,*[64] the court found that three things should never be considered trial strategy. The first is whether or not to present mitigation in a death case. The second is that a client has an absolute right to testify, and the third is whether or not the defendant will take a plea of insanity or claim insanity as a defense at trial. When a decision is part of the trial strategy, the lawyer maintains discretion and the defendant will usually have a difficult time claiming ineffective assistance of counsel.

Scientific Evidence

Popular culture has influenced jurors to the point that some judges now advise jurors of the unrealistic nature of shows like "*CSI*" and "*Law and Order*." The first myth spread by these shows is the idea that DNA testing is available in all cases. Although DNA can be found in almost any cell in the body, it is present for testing in only about 10% of all cases. Fingerprint analysis is also problematic because jurors incorrectly believe that it is available everywhere and that it is scientifically infallible. When it comes to fingerprint evidence, the first obstacle is finding a fingerprint clear enough to analyze. The second issue is that fingerprint

[62] 466 U.S. 688 (1984).
[63] *Id.*
[64] 539 U.S. 510 (2003).

analysts have different standards depending on the examiner and the jurisdiction[65]. Finally, fingerprint analysts have their own biases; different factors such as showing them a suspect's prints or giving them possible matches may influence them to give incorrect conclusions.[66] Although scientists, other expert examiners are only human, and extraneous circumstances sometimes influence their evaluations as well.[67]

In general, flawed scientific evidence is a dangerous form of evidence,[68] because jurors find it so compelling. The false sense of assurance provided by this type of evidence is difficult to dismantle, and it is tough to dissuade jurors from their faith in what is often nothing but scientific jargon or junk science. In fact, the National Academy of Sciences concluded that no other scientific method of identification other than DNA testing can reliably connect a physical sample with a suspect. All of the other types of testing are subject to biases and ill-defined subjective standards that can produce error.[69]

Cell Confessions

Sometimes statements of admission come from cellmates or other inmates. Undoubtedly, there are times when defendants make the mistake of admitting crimes to those around them; however, frequently these situations are more complex than an honest confession from one inmate to another. For example, at times the prosecution will approach the inmate to let him know that they are looking for a confession from a fellow prisoner. The 'snitch' then becomes an agent of the state. The snitch will often exchange the acquired information for perks such as early release. *U.S. v. Mesiah*[70] held that the Sixth Amendment

---

[65], Jennifer L. Mnookin , *The Achilles' Heel of Fingerprints*, TRUTH IN JUSTICE (May 29, 2004), http://truthinjustice.org/fingerprint-flaws.htm.

[66]Linda Geddess, M*iscarriage of Justice Points to Fingerprint Flaws*, NEW SCIENTIST (Dec. 28, 2011), http://www.newscientist.com/article/mg21228442.600-miscarriage-of-justice-points-to-fingerprint-flaws.html.

[67] Mnookin, *supra* note 65.

[68] Chris Fabricant, Director of Strategic Litigation. Innocence Project, Inc. "As the DNA exonerations have revealed, the misapplication of forensic science has been a leading cause of wrongful convictions".

[69] Jonathan Jones, *Forensic Tools: What's Reliable and What's Not-So-Scientific*, PBS.ORG (Apr. 17, 2012, 9:48 PM), http://www.pbs.org/wgbh/pages/frontline/criminal-justice/real-csi/forensic-tools-whats-reliable-and-whats-not-so-scientific/.

[70] 377 U.S. 201 (1964).

prohibits the government from obtaining incriminating statements from the defendant without counsel after the right to counsel has attached. Decisions such as this limit the government's ability to take advantage of a defendant by using deceptive techniques such as a confidential informant.

Inmates also approach lawyers and prosecutors claiming to have heard confessions from cellmates. These inmates are invariably looking to make a deal in exchange for their testimony regarding these confessions. There is no legal ban on this type of testimony. However, if the inmate receives compensation from the government in the form of a reduced sentence, etc. his testimony carries little weight and credibility. With a strong cross, the jury may disregard this inmate's testimony (let's call him what he is – a snitch). The snitch has a strong motive to lie and very little credibility. Intensive investigation into the background of this snitch may reveal previous behavior of this sort, previous "false" testimony, promises that were made in exchange for the testimony and more. Snitches are common occurrences in innocence cases. It is striking how often juries believe them or maybe it is how bad the lawyers cross the snitches that is striking.

Prosecutorial Misconduct

The duty of the prosecution should be to seek truth. Unfortunately, truth finding is sometimes overshadowed by the desire for a conviction. The government has a continuing duty to provide the defense with any and all evidence that could be exculpatory or lead to exculpatory evidence.[71] A discovery of prosecutorial misconduct of this type would allow the defendant to re-open his case because it would constitute new evidence. Note, that there is usually a time bar for appeals on such grounds. Again, it may depend on your jurisdiction.

[71] *See* Brady v. Maryland, 373 U.S. 83 (1963).

Chapter Ten

Investigation

Now that you have a case that meets the screening criteria, it is time to investigate. Whether you are looking for new evidence or DNA, a number of things need to be done. In almost every case you will need to: get the trial and appellate transcripts, speak to the appellate and trial attorneys, speak to all available family[72], obtain all previously filed post-conviction motions, speak to your client on the phone or in person, research any legal issues raised, talk to the trial and appellate prosecutor(s), make an inventory of what documents you have and what you need, make a "cast of characters" and their roles, make two timelines (one for the crime and one for the case), and investigate the police, prosecutors, and witnesses (backgrounds, motives, criminal history, relationships).

1. Obtain the Trial and Appellate Transcripts, all previously filed Post-Conviction Motions, and Outline them all

Get the trial and appellate court transcripts, post-conviction motions, depositions, police reports and all documents prepared up until you receive the case; these constitute one of your primary sources of information. This is also one of the very first things you should do when you begin to investigate a case because it is difficult to know much about your case without transcripts and reports. If you have difficulty obtaining these documents, continue to work on the case until you locate and receive them. In the meantime, keep working on other avenues of the case; for example, you can conduct legal research or call the client's family for more information.

Where can you get these transcripts? They are at the Clerk's office, but hopefully you do not have to get them from there. Many Clerks' offices charge up to $1.00 per page for making copies of pages of transcripts and the court file.

---

[72] You must get your supervisor's authorization before speaking to any family. You must also be aware that not all family members are friendly. Often another family member is the victim and the family is not trying to help your client. Contact with adversarial family members may still need to be made, but with great care, sensitivity, and thought.

These transcripts can be thousands of pages long. Remember our common denominator? Almost all innocence programs have money problems. Many inmates have their own transcripts and they can mail them to you. You may also be able to get the transcripts from the inmate's family members or prior counsel. If all else fails, perhaps your program can buy a scanner. This is a handheld device that scans one page at a time to a jump drive. You can go to the courthouse and scan everything you need out of the court file and upload it to a computer. Beware that some Clerk's offices will only let an attorney do this (sorry, directors); nevertheless, it is likely that a certified student could do it.

A note about trial and appellate transcripts and depositions: you must outline them. This is tedious work but you may find diamonds in the details. Outlining involves reading the documents line by line, taking each fact, and extracting it by noting the page and line of its location in the document. Outlining works best by writing the fact on one side of the paper and the page and line number on the opposite side and so forth. This procedure is necessary to tease out inconsistencies in testimony as well as for impeachment at hearings or trials. See the appendix for an example of an outline of a transcript.

2. Speak to the Trial and Appellate Attorneys

The following list of actions is not in any particular order. If your case meets the screening criteria and you have therefore done substantial investigation, then all of these actions should be performed before most cases are denied.[73] Let's start with phone calls. Here are some general rules regarding any innocence program phone call:

1) Obtain your supervisor's consent.
2) Send your supervisor an outline of what you intend to say or information you intend to obtain.
3) If applicable, arrange a time when your supervisor can be present for the call.
4) Secure a private and quiet area to make the call.
5) Allow enough time to make the call so that you are not rushed.

---

[73] Reasonable minds can differ. In particular, some projects may feel that it is not in the client's best interest to contact him or her by phone early in the case, because this may get the inmate's hopes up unnecessarily. There is merit in this position.

6) Always clearly identify yourself and the purpose of your call at the beginning of your call.[74]
7) Try not to read from notes during your call. In other words, relax (to the extent possible) and have a natural conversation.
8) Conversely, DO make an outline of what you need to cover during the call.
9) Have a drink of water with you during the call if you need a moment or get nervous.
10) Never hesitate to ask the person on the phone to give you just a moment (then look at your outline or take a sip of water.)
11) Always start any phone interview by letting the person speak a bit while you listen to whatever they need to say.
12) Keep confidentiality in mind at all times.
13) Do not call from your cell or home phone thereby giving the person you are calling your personal phone number.
14) Be confident but not arrogant.
15) Do not give answers to questions when you are not sure of the answer – say you will find out. If the question asked of you is legal and your supervisor is not present it may be best to tell them that you will let them know in your next communication. When you are a student you must be careful to not risk practicing law without a license.

Calling the client's prior counsel can be intimidating at times. This is normal. You may have to call these attorneys several times before you get through; be persistent. They may have information you need. Your case may have been handled by these attorneys many years ago (10 to 20 years even), so it is not unusual for them to have a foggy recollection. Often, however, they want to have a bad memory because they want nothing to do with your client. Ask the attorney very detailed and factual questions. Not many attorneys can completely forget the kind of cases that innocence programs deal with: murders and rapes. The attorney you are speaking to lost the case, so be sensitive but press on. Perhaps, just to get out of talking to you, he will offer to send you his entire file. If you have a cooperative attorney who feels bad about the loss, she may explain to you what

[74] I have made the mistake of not doing this and the witness I was speaking to thought I was a prosecutor for most of the deposition. I was a new public defender. Boy, was this witness mad when I finally identified myself! This rule applies to phone calls, interviews, depositions, court appearances, and almost anytime you open your mouth.

she would have done differently, what was not investigated or who was not interviewed. If the information is not volunteered, those questions need to be asked.

3. Speak to Your Client

Speaking to your client on the phone or in person can be one of the most rewarding experiences in an innocence program. It can be profoundly sad or it can encourage great optimism. He or she is also your best source of information. Special considerations for speaking to clients whether in person or on the phone are:

1) Always remember your client is probably scared even if he is acting upset or angry.
2) Remember it is your job to stay calm and patient (even if you think your client is a homicidal maniac).
3) Remember that building trust takes time, and your client may be embarrassed, remorseful, and angry, making opening up to you difficult at first.
4) Always LISTEN. Ask follow-up questions even if not pertinent to the investigation to demonstrate to your client that you were listening and that you care.
5) Never promise outcomes to a client.
6) Do not treat clients like they are stupid; treat them with courtesy and respect.
7) Use simple – non-lawyer – language with your client.[75]
8) Go over client-attorney confidentiality (depends on stage of proceedings).
9) Let your client vent, complain, be angry or get anything off of his chest that he needs to.
10) Remember to ask about your client's health, well-being, family and general personal details. Let him know that you and the program care about him as a person.
11) If you are on the phone and not at the prison remember all of the conditions in section two of this Chapter.
12) You will also need to schedule this phone call in advance. Depending on the prison, it is usually at least 48 hours in advance. You must first

[75] In fact, it's good advice to trash the lawyer talk – period.

call the prison to find out when you may talk to your client. You should also have your client's corrections number available. Once they give you a time, most prisons require a fax confirmation of the phone appointment. It is very important that you add this on the fax: ***please be advised that all information discussed during the phone interview is protected by attorney-client privilege. Please ensure that the inmate is provided with a non-monitored and non-recorded phone line and that the inmate is provided privacy for the phone call.*** Once you are on the phone, ask the client if he is alone or if someone is listening, and never be too confident that the line is not monitored. A sample of a fax confirmation is found in the appendix. Prison requirements differ by prison and by location. It often seems the same prison's requirements differ by time of day. Therefore, always call the prison and inquire about their requirements for setting up a telephone attorney interview with your client.

13) If you are in prison: Be polite to the corrections officers; they think they can do anything and they usually can. You do not want to make the trip to the prison for nothing by getting thrown out. Follow all of the prison rules. However, insist on your rights such as actually getting to see your client in the same room. Also, leave your knife, gun or machete at home. If you are a female (or male) do not wear open toed shoes, wraparound skirt, or an underwire bra (this is not a joke)[76].
14) If you are interviewing your client in a team, designate one of you to take the lead so the interview will flow like a conversation.
15) Review the list in section one (realizing not all are possible if your client is in prison – you can't offer him coffee or a quiet place). In every way possible, however, your client should be treated with the same respect and dignity as a potential client at a plush high-priced law firm.
16) Once the client is ready for specific questions be very detailed.

1. How was the client identified?
2. What type of scientific evidence was used at trial and how was it obtained?
3. What type of interrogation tactics did the police use to obtain information?

[76] The underwire bra will set off the metal detectors and corrections will make you remove your bra. Yes, humiliating.

4. Was he satisfied with the legal representation that he received? Why or why not?
5. Is there any new evidence that could be discovered that would shed new light on the case?
6. Are there witnesses who could provide useful information?

Above all, after you have contact with your client, keep in touch with him. You can do this by phone calls and by letters. You are likely the only person in his corner, the only one who cares. Regardless of whether you obtain an exoneration, he is likely to cherish your attention and concern. Your effort is likely to be appreciated beyond what we can imagine. As mentioned earlier, some programs hesitate to contact clients early in the case so as not to give him or her false hope. It may also give the client the impression the attorney-client relationship has formed. In any conversations you have with your client you should always clarify the status of the attorney-client relationship. You should also obtain consent to speak to third parties for purposes of furthering your investigation on the case. The point at which the attorney-client relationship attaches is something that your program and supervisors will decide. If you do speak to a client when it is unclear whether the case will move forward, please keep this in mind. A client who faces dying in prison could be devastated when his last resort turns down his case. It is important not to give your client false hope. It is wise to repeat that you remain unsure of the future of the case.

4. Speak To All Available Family Members Or Possible Witnesses

There are ethical rules surrounding who you may speak to about the case. Make sure to discuss these rules with your supervisor. Generally, you may not attempt to interview anyone who is represented by counsel in the same matter. However, you may call that person's lawyer to arrange an interview. This could occur if you are attempting to interview your client's co-defendant. If the person you are interviewing has no legal counsel and asks you for legal advice (or your supervisor for legal advice), you may not give it.

A common and very touchy example of this is when you are dealing with recanting witnesses. For example, you may be interviewing the grown step-daughter of your client. Your client has been convicted of raping her when she was 12 years old. You have every reason to believe she is about to recant and admit it never happened. Then she asks the dreaded question "Can I get in trouble with the law if I admit I lied back then?" For you the room is spinning. Do you really care that much about those silly rules at this moment? I am sorry but you do. You must have a pre-planned response for these questions. Many directors of innocence programs consider the following answer ethical and appropriate, "Ma'am, I am not allowed to give you any legal advice, but from what I have personally seen, I have never seen anything happen to a person in that position". However, I personally know directors of innocence programs who have had recanting witnesses be charged with perjury. It depends upon the jurisdiction. Many would say the above statement crosses the boundary of ethically appropriate and goes too far. Again, you must discuss ethics with your supervisor as these issues can be complicated.

Another approach would be to simply advise her you are not allowed to give her legal advice, and ask her why speaking the truth should hinge on that question when an innocent person is in prison for many years. You could tell her she should hire a lawyer, which I often recommend and is the ethically most conservative option. This must be considered seriously and sometimes must be done. The moral of this paragraph is that dealing with recanting witnesses is a sensitive matter that requires much advance planning and thought as well as thinking on your feet.

Beware as there are two types of family members, hostile and friendly. You may be charged with determining who is who. Frequently your client will be able to tell you. This is why I normally suggest speaking with your client early and often. He or she usually knows who is angry and who is supportive. Also, there is a place on most applications for the client to suggest witnesses, friends and family for you to call. It is likely that these are the friendly characters. However, never assume too much. Always be on guard for a furious lion on the other end of the line when you expected a sympathetic kitten. Although these calls with outraged kin may be highly unpleasant, they can be very informative. Some tips for handling angry phone calls:

1) Never yell back or scream or use profanity no matter how rude or profane the caller becomes.
2) The expression "I understand" spoken in a soft and calm voice is useful and sounds sympathetic but does not betray your client in any way.
3) Be silent and let the person complain away.
4) If you want to get more information, you might say "I want to understand your position – can you explain to me further how (insert here the information you want)."
5) Do not tape anyone without their permission – I advise against it even with consent. This is a procedure that differs by clinic so please consult your director or supervisor.

6) If the person does not have useful information for your case and is simply angry with you or your client and you need to get off the phone you might try, "I understand, but my job is to represent Joe. I am sure you can respect that, and I really have to get off the phone if you are going to yell at me and insult me". Instead of abruptly hanging up – say to the person, "I am hanging up now" and say this a few times. Do this only if the person is being unruly and abusive to you.

Assuming you are speaking to a friendly witness, many of the same rules apply as when speaking to your client. Make an outline of the information you want and be as detailed as possible. Establishing a rapport is important because, if the case becomes a case for innocence, these witnesses may be significant, and you will need a positive relationship with them. It is always essential to be polite and respectful, and to listen to anyone you interview. What if your mind goes completely blank in a state of nerves, chronic fatigue and cluelessness? (Anyone who says this has never happened to them is surely lying.)

Step 1: take a sip of water and see if that relaxes you enough to remember what you were going to ask – if not go to step 2:

Step 2: Ask the witness/client to give you a moment whether you are on phone or in person. If the interview is in person, step out for a moment (bring your outline) and go to the bathroom and splash some water on your face and look at your outline. Throw up if you need to.[77] If you are wearing a lot of make-up, skip the water part. If you still are blocking on what you were supposed to ask this person go to step 3:

Step 3: Turn the interview over to your supervisor or teammate if they were also in the room. If they are also unprepared and don't know what to ask go to step 4:

Step 4: Go back in the room or get back on the phone and just start talking to the witness/client about anything at all: How is his health? Has he been eating? What does he want to talk about? Eventually you will remember and get your groove back. If you don't...go to step 5:

Step 5: Tell the witness/client: "time's up" and that you will schedule another interview or call very soon and it was super nice to talk to him. Go to step 6:

---

[77] Try not to get vomit on your clothing – if you do, skip to step five.

Step 6: Go home and repeat to yourself: *Don't sweat the petty things and don't pet the sweaty things.* Go to step 7:

Step 7: Take a nap.

The point being, this is no big deal and happens to every lawyer. It happens in interviews, in depositions, and most horribly, in court. If you are prepared, a blank brain can't hurt you because you will know your facts to make it right. You will have an outline to jog your memory and save you and your client. Lawyers don't get embarrassed; we just allow our egos to get bruised because they are too big and in the way of everything. Plus, your supervising attorney should be there to save you. In fact, you may learn more from the days you mess everything up than you will from the days you do everything perfectly. The client is protected by your director and supervisors.

5. Talk to the Trial and the Appellate Prosecutors

There is not much to add in this section about interviewing. It is significant for you to be aware that the vast majority of prosecutors to whom you speak are firmly convinced of your client's guilt and will treat you like you are daft to even suggest that your client might be innocent. You should expect condescension, arrogance, and irritation. Even on that shiny day in the future when you might present incontrovertible evidence of your client's innocence to the prosecutor (e.g., DNA of another person), the prosecutor often scoffs that something is wrong with the DNA test. Do not expect a pleasant interaction here.

6. Do any Necessary Legal Research

This part of investigating an innocence case is easy to brush over. The fact is that almost every potential innocence case has issues that need to be researched. This is a vast area that is very new and changing at light speed. No one can say with confidence that we are up to date on the law in the area of innocence as it changes so rapidly. In each and every case that makes it to investigation, there should be a list made of "legal issue spotting." This is a list of issues that need to be researched.

7. Make an inventory of what documents you have and what you need

At this point in your investigation, you may need to go back to the beginning of Chapter Ten, because it may not make much sense to make an inventory until you have completed all of the above and have obtained as many documents as you can. This inventory should be clear enough for students and attorneys to read and understand. You should have a clear idea why you need the documents you list. By this point in the investigation, you should have a holistic idea of what the case is about and where it is going. At this juncture, a student or colleague should be able to say to you: "Hey, how's that Peeble case going?" and you should be able to rattle off its problem areas, its strengths, the client's family history, and more.

8. Make a "cast of characters" and describe their roles

This also cannot be done until you know the role each person plays. Your interviews will need to be mostly complete. By creating a "cast of characters" you will remember the participants better. Remember that you are likely to have more than one case so recalling the details of each one can be a challenge. Make this cast perform a real show and inform others who may read this document of the real action going on in your case. Remember, we are lawyers, even though you are investigating, it is never too early to start developing a theme for your case. (yes – post-conviction motions and hearings must have themes!)

9. Make 3 timelines: two for the crime and one for the case's procedural history

Why three timelines you say? Make three timelines: two for the crime and one for the case's procedural history. With regard to the two crime timelines, if your client is innocent his timeline is different than that of the crime. We must compare the two. The third procedural history timeline simply details the legal/procedural history without including case facts.

10. Investigate police, prosecutors, witnesses (backgrounds, motives, criminal history, relationships)

Here is where you think "*CSI-MIAMI*" or "*Days of our Lives*" whichever is more your style. If you watch "*The Simpsons*" or "*The Walking Dead*" it can still work. Who was having an affair with whom? Where is the motive? Who was secretly a drug addict? Maybe Helen's baby is Jim's not Joe's and Jim found out? Maybe Mary is still secretly married to Mick but is in love with Donald? How do you find out these things? Jim is not going to tell you. You will often be seeking records: hospital records, jail records, work records. A subpoena is magical but also has side effects like angering the recipient and winding you up in court to show good cause for its service. A good rule of thumb is to try to get your information in any other (legal) way you can before resorting to a subpoena. First, just ask for the documents – you never know. If that doesn't work, look around for people who might already have a legal right to the information and see if you can persuade them to get the information for you.

Sometimes you do have to use a subpoena. You must have good cause to serve a subpoena and, as with everything discussed in this book, you must have your supervisor's authorization before attempting to serve one. Since you are not yet a lawyer, your supervisor will need to sign the subpoena. In some jurisdictions, you will need to contact a company that serves subpoenas. Find out if your program uses a particular one. The law usually states a reasonable period of time must be given, without defining reasonable. You should remember it will take five working days for the subpoena to be served by a process company and then the recipient needs the time to comply. In other jurisdictions, the sheriff will serve indigent defendants, and in some locations any adult may serve a subpoena, in which case an innocence program investigator, student or director could serve the subpoena and it would not take five days as would the process company. A subpoena must be very specific as to what you are requesting. If your request is too broad it may be stricken. The subpoena also may not ask for an unreasonable number of items or put an undue burden on its recipient. Be sure to allow a reasonable amount of time for the recipient to comply with the request. An example of a typical subpoena can be found in the appendix.

Chapter Eleven

DNA Basics

If you are in a program that accepts DNA cases, you must look for any biological material that could be tested for DNA. In this instance you must locate the biological material that contains the DNA of the perpetrator on it. Finding the biological material that could contain the DNA is often a challenge. DNA is not found only in semen or blood as was once thought; it can be found in any cell in the body. Technology is improving so rapidly that we cannot ignore the possibility of detection and testing of DNA on almost any human sample. For example, DNA science can now retrieve testable DNA from the perpetrator's fingerprint or nail scraping. The future possibilities are endless, so search thoroughly because you never know what may be viable for testing. Today, we have a nationwide databank that stores convicted felons,' DNA called CODIS. If you obtain DNA results from a crime scene that does not match your client, you may even identify the real culprit by entering the DNA in CODIS and finding a match.

Where is this biological evidence being held? Does it still exist? You will need to find out the public records rule in your jurisdiction. Most states have such a law that allows the public to view or know the whereabouts of evidence in criminal cases. A sample letter that requests the documentation of the existence of biological evidence or proof of its destruction is found in the appendix. Once you have located the biological evidence you can consider filing a motion for DNA testing with your supervisors. This is a decision to be made carefully along with your director or professor.

DNA testing that does not match your client is not always enough to obtain an exoneration. The prosecutor may argue the DNA was yet a third party's DNA. Even though you will have done elimination testing (for example in a rape you would also test the DNA of the husband or boyfriend), the prosecutor could still claim that the victim had multiple sexual partners that day. Redundancy is when you find the same DNA (not your client's) in other incriminating areas attaching that person's DNA to the crime. This makes it much more likely for your client to be exonerated. Of course, locating the true culprit through CODIS is the best case scenario.

DNA in the body:[78]

- DNA is a nucleic acid that controls the development and functions of all humans.
- There are two kinds of DNA:
    - Nuclear – found in semen, blood, saliva, sweat, hair root.
    - Non-nuclear (Mitochondrial) – hair, bones, fingernails.
- Nucleus – 46 chromosomes – 23 from mother (egg) and 23 from father (sperm).
- DNA testing works because in nuclear testing the pairs match up differently from person to person.
- One member of a pair of genes that is located in a specific place on a chromosome is called an allele.
- These codings are passed from parent to child.

Old DNA testing: RFLP

- RFLP is not used anymore.
- RFLP was not very sensitive and required large amounts of biological material to test but was very discriminating

Current DNA Testing: STR, Y-STR, MiniSTR, and Mitochondrial

- <u>STR (Short Tandem Repeat)</u>
    - Much more sensitive.
    - Number of markers makes it highly discriminating.
    - Determines sex.
    - Compatible with CODIS.

- <u>Y-STR – Y chromosome DNA Testing</u>
    - Tests for DNA in the Y chromosome.
    - Useful for samples with DNA from multiple males.

[78] *Introduction to DNA Testing*, Seth Miller, Executive Director, Innocence Project of Florida and Olga Akselrod, Staff Attorney, The Innocence Project, Innocence Network Conference, Cincinnati, Ohio, April 9, 2011. This section is lifted directly from my notes which were taken from Olga and Seth's power-point. Thank you, Seth and Olga.

  - Useful for samples with either little female DNA or lots of female DNA.
  - Not as discriminating as STR because paternally inherited.
  - Not compatible with CODIS.
  - Can't be used where the paternal relative or female is alternative suspect.

- MiniSTR
  - Good for degraded samples.
  - More sensitive, so less DNA is needed.
  - Good alternative to STR if sample is small.
  - Because so sensitive can produce mixed profiles, including contaminants.

- Mitochondrial DNA testing
  - Good for hairs and bones.
  - Maternally inherited so less discriminating.
  - Not compatible with CODIS.
  - Mixtures difficult to interpret.

Did any of that make sense? Do not worry if it did not. You will have many people who do understand it supporting you when you get to the point of arguing a DNA motion. Unless your state lab is high-quality and you have a good relationship with them, it is often advised that, if finances permit, you use a private lab. With a private lab you may have more accurate results, a better relationship with the lab technician and hence a better understanding of your results.

Chapter Twelve

Remedies

This section is brief as this book is not the place to teach post-conviction law. As stated earlier, your first call to action in an innocence program is to learn and understand your jurisdiction's post-conviction law and procedures. It is there that you will find the remedies for the wrongfully convicted. Most of the time, a DNA test indicating that your client is not the perpetrator will defeat any time limitations and get your client into court. Sometimes DNA alone is not enough for an exoneration, e.g., if there were multiple perpetrators or if, in a rape case, the victim had intercourse with other men recently. Most states have a state rule of procedure allowing for a motion for post-conviction relief if it is filed within a number of years from the time the appeal became final.

If the judge summarily denies a motion for post-conviction relief without a hearing, you may appeal the ruling, not on the merits, but on the judge's decision not to provide you with a hearing. If the state judge provides you a hearing and you lose, you may appeal that in the district court. Once you have exhausted all of your state court remedies, you may file a habeas corpus motion in federal court under 28 USC 2254 within one year of the state court's final appeal. If you lose this motion, you may petition for a writ of certiorari to the Supreme Court of the United States.

Chapter Thirteen

Documentation

Documentation should have been Chapter One. I made it Chapter Thirteen because you will be cursed if you do not document ***everything***. Hotels don't even have a thirteenth floor to protect you from getting cursed. This book has a Chapter Thirteen to make a point. You will not know what is going on with your cases if you do not do a good job documenting them. Problematically, your director or supervisor may not be updated properly and fully about your client. Even worse, your successor student will not know up from down on the case and the client will be damaged. Have I scared you? Documenting is not hard. It is simple: simple to do and simple to forget to do. Every program has a different method of documentation, but the concept remains the same; document everything you do (really ***everything***). Some innocence programs use folders and on the front you must write everything you do with a date. This is the classic way. I am betting that your supervisor will not be satisfied with excuses like "the file was in the office" when items have not been updated, even when utilizing the classic style. Other programs use high tech software. You have no excuses when you go high tech. These software programs can be accessed from anywhere; any computer, your car, your phone, in the yard, etc. So if you call the client's second cousin on a Sunday night, and she doesn't answer, you can access your client's file right then and document the attempted contact instead of waiting until Monday morning. Your particular innocence program will have specific procedures for using the software, like passwords, where to put your name, where to put these updates, etc. It is your obligation to find out and understand how the documentation procedures work as priority one and a half. If you recall, learning the post-conviction law was priority one[79]. Now remember, the rule in Chapter Thirteen is: document ***everything***, or you will be cursed.

---

[79] Of course the best interests of your client are always overall the top priority.

Conclusion

Chances are that if you are reading this conclusion, you have decided to participate in an innocence program. I commend you. I hope this little book was helpful. If it was not helpful I hope it helped you get to sleep on restless nights. This book is intended to be a reference and to be used as many times as needed. It is a guide book. Each chapter provides just enough information to point you the right direction. Please do not rely on this book alone for any topic as it is intended to give you a good running start with some helpful advice and a solid reference to return to whenever needed. You also now know a little something about almost anything involving innocence work. At your next cocktail party you will have something substantial to add to the conversation if any innocence topic comes up instead of pretending to suddenly need to use the restroom. As a bonus, this book is lightweight and small compared to your other back-breaking text books, it's easy to carry in your backpack or purse, you can take it with you everywhere you go, perhaps its best feature.

Some of the suggestions in the book may work for you and others may not. Much of it is personal. Every program is as diverse as the clients they serve. If you worked in or are working in an innocence program, I hope you know that every little bit of work you do is meaningful and appreciated. It is hard to stay motivated at times, but always remember that it is your work and commitment that brings us one step closer to freeing an innocent person who is now suffering.

Appendix:
Forms and Templates

Sample Confidentiality Agreement

I, [Print Name] ________________________________, hereby acknowledge that by participating in the [insert name of Innocence Program]; I will have access to confidential documents related to the [Program] and its work with [name of State] inmates.

I understand that I have an obligation to protect the confidentiality of all such documents. I also understand that trust and a full exchange of information among the members of the [Program], the inmates and their lawyers is critical to the effort of the [Program] to assist the inmates; in some cases, such confidential information may determine whether an innocent inmate is freed from prison.

I understand when I obtain such confidential information, I owe a strict duty of confidentiality and loyalty to the inmate who is the subject of the information I receive.

Accordingly, I agree not to divulge such confidences and information to persons outside of the [Program], unless expressly permitted to do so by associated faculty. I also agree to hold in the strictest confidence any information I learn about other inmates from other members of the [Program].

Finally, I understand that, through the [Program], I may have access to attorney work-product in the form of manuals and manuscripts, etc. discussing strategies for pursuing innocence claims. I agree not to divulge the content of such material to any agent of the State, including law enforcement officers, or members of the office of a district attorney or attorney general.

Signed: ____

Dated this ____ day of ___________________, 20____.

Sample: Examples of Outlining

#1 Trial Transcript (Excel)

Make sure to note when direct/cross/redirect/recross occurs and who the attorney is

Each line contains ONE fact

Each fact should have corresponding line and page numbers, even if they are on multiple pages

Each witness has their own tab and they are sequential in the order of the trial

Make a tab for key points in the trial

	A	B
1	**DIRECT - Ms. Vergos**	
2	Detective with Pasco Sheriff's Office	311; 1-2
3	Been with the office for 10 years	311; 3-5
4	Was in Major Crimes for 4 years	311; 13-14
5	Major crimes investise anything from child abuse to homicides	311; 16-17
6	Did 50-100 investigations of a child's physical or sexual abuse	311; 18-24
7	Jan 29 2007 received case for investigation against Jason	312; 9-12
8	Case came because assigned by supervisor	312; 13-14
9	Initial report taken by School Resource Officer	312; 15-16
10	Corporal Journer was the one who did the initial report	312; 18-19
11	After Journer finished initial report, forwarded it over to him	312; 20-22
12	Began investigation on 29th of Jan	312, 313; 24-25, 1-2
13	Did not conduct interview with Samantha	313; 9-11
14	Because assigned to another investigation and knew couldn't make the appt that had set with the famuly so sent hem to Child Protective Team for an interview	313; 13-17
15	Child Protective Team specialize in child forensic interviews and also on occasion do medical exams on children	313 19-21
16	Sent Samantha to get a medical examination	313; 22-24
17	February 28 sent to get medical exam	313-314; 24-25, 1
18	Delay between report and exam based on information obtained through the investigation	314; 2-6
19	Exam tries to find any physical evidence, forensic physical evidence that may be present due to some type of assauly	314; 9-11
20	Options after finish investigation are inactivate it on the type of information obtained, can refer it to SA's office for review and prosecution, can make a physical arrest	314; 20-24
21	Referred the instant investigation to SA's office for their review	315; 1-2
22	Was not the person who mede the physical arrest after warrant was issued	315; 9-11
23		
24	**CROSS- Mr. Watson**	
25	Wasn't present when this happened	315; 21-23
26	Base investigation on witness statements and evidence	315; 24-25
27	No physical evidence in the case	316; 2-4
28	Samantha questioned Jan 31	316; 8-9
29	Jason questioned Feb 21	316; 10-11
30	Delay was because of another investigation, trying to manage both	316; 12-17
31	Finished investigation before March 2007	316; 18-20
32	Unsure when warrant issued	316; 22-23

Yvonne Clapp | Christopher Beaman | James Meissner | PROFFER - Christina Mixoks | Eric Petti | STATE RESTS

Ready

#2 Deposition (Word)

Summary of Deposition: JOHN SMITH (May 14, 2007)

Facts	Page: Line
Met with defendant May 12, 2000	10; 1-2
Saw defendant had gun – Colt 45	10; 5
Mr. Smith was intoxicated	11; 3
Had 6 Bud Lights in the afternoon	11; 3-4
Finished drinking at 4	11; 7
Defendant came to Mr. Smith's house around 6	11; 9
No one else was home	11; 11-12
Talked about nothing in particular, decided to go for a ride	11; 14-17
Met up with Johnny Boy at the 7-11	12; 4-5
Johnny Boy said that he had a job for them to do	12; 10
Did not say what the job was	12; 14
Mr. Smith did not know what he was referring to	12; 17
Didn't ask, just sat back and went for the ride	12; 20

Sample Screening Sheet

Defendant Name: ______________________________________

Student Screener: ______________________________________

Date Screened: ____

Checklist (some of these items may not be applicable to your Program):

	YES	NO
Is Defendant claiming actual innocence?	____	____
Defendant is not claiming self-defense.	____	____
Defendant has exhausted all appellate remedies	____	____
Not a death penalty case	____	____
At least 10 years left on Defendant's sentence	____	____
Defendant does not currently have counsel	____	____

ALL OF THE ABOVE SHOULD BE CHECKED "YES" TO BE ELIGIBLE

Date Defendant's judgment and sentence became final: ___________

Any possible "newly discovered evidence" – discuss:

____

____

____

Any biological evidence? Describe:

____

____

ACCEPT _____ DENY _____ FURTHER INVESTIGATION _____

SEE PAGE 2 for explanatory memo.

SCREENING CONLCUSION SUPPORTING MEMORANDUM

[Insert name of Innocence Program]

Defendant Name: ____

Student Screener: ____

Date Screened: ____

Screening Decision: ____

1. Case Summary (factual)
2. Legal Support with Case Law (may require research)
3. Action Taken (e.g. denial sent)
4. To do list (research on topic needed, phone calls, be specific)
5. Attach more pages if needed
6. Type only – File appropriately

Sample Referral Letter

[Date]

[Name]

[Address]

Re: Request for Legal Assistance

Dear [Name]:

We have received your letter that you provided. We regret to inform you that we cannot assist you on your case since we only review South Florida cases. We take no position on the merits of any claim you raise. Please contact the Innocence Project nearest you:

[Contact information of referral State. *See* WCP Innocence Project listing.]

Sincerely,

[Name of Innocence Program]

[Address]

[Email]

Sample Termination Letter

[Date]

[Name]

[Address]

Re: Request for Legal Assistance

Dear [Name]:

We have received your letter [or application, etc.] that you provided. We regret to inform you that we cannot assist you on your case. We take no position on the merits of any claim you raise.

Sincerely,

[Insert name of Innocence Program]

[Address]

[Email]

Sample Solicitation Response Letter

[Date]

[Name]

[Address]

Re: Request for Legal Assistance

Dear [Name]:

We recently received your letter requesting assistance. Please complete the enclosed forms. We will review it as soon as possible. However, we review requests in the order in which they arrive, so it may be several months before we are able to review your application.

It is very important that you read the last page of the form carefully and that you sign your name. By signing the last page, you are giving the [insert name of Innocence Program] permission to research your case further by obtaining court documents, laboratory results, police records, and other information we may need. We will need this permission if and when we are able to help you. Also, we must know if there is currently a lawyer or group reviewing the case for you.

We are not consenting to provide you with representation and we recommend that you obtain legal counsel if you are able.

There are time limits that apply to some post-conviction relief claims. If your direct appeal was finalized recently, you should contact a lawyer to make sure that you file a claim within the time limit.

We are not attorneys, but are law students who research claims of actual innocence. Thank you for your patience and you will hear from us if and when we are able to assist you.

Sincerely,

[Name of Innocence Program]

[Address]

[Email]

Sample Application (space for inmate's response condensed)

Application For Assistance
[insert name of Innocence Program]

A National Innocence Project Affiliate
(Please use ink)

Please answer the following questions as thoroughly as possible and sign the last page. The information you provide with us will help us determine whether or not we will be able to help you prove your innocence. We are only able to accept cases from persons convicted in [insert State] and from persons who are not already legally represented. We do not review cases [insert categories outside scope of review]. The [insert name of Innocence Program] will use your answers to these questions to see if your case is one that we can accept. If you do not understand a question please write: "I do not understand this question." If you do not know the answer to a question that you think you should answer, please write: "I do not know." It is imperative that you answer as completely and truthfully as possible. Failure to do so will result in the denial of your application for assistance by the [insert name of Innocence Program].

Today's Date: ___________________________

Name: ____ Inmate ID#_______________

Date of Birth: ___________________ County of Conviction: _____________________

Name of Prison: ____

Address: ______________________________ City: _________ State: __ Zip Code: ___________

Date Sentenced: ____________________
Length of Sentence: ____________________

Sample Application (Con't)

ABOUT YOU AND YOUR CASE

What is your first language?

1. Do use any other languages? If so please list them:

2. Highest grade you finished in school?

3. Date of Incident:

4. Place of Incident:

5. Were you present at the scene of crime?

6. Date of Arrest:

7. Place of Arrest:

8. What crimes were you **charged** with from this arrest? (List them all).

9. What crimes were you **convicted** of from this arrest? (List them all).

Do you claim to be innocent for all of the above crimes? If no, for which do you claim to be innocent?

Do you currently have legal representation? If so, list attorney's name.

B. Briefly describe the facts of your case. Include the role the State says you played in the crime, dates, and details of the crime for which you were convicted. (please include additional sheets if necessary).

Sample Application (Con't)

Please use a copy of your Department of Corrections Timesheet to answer the following 2 questions:

How much time were you sentenced to serve for each one of the crimes (please list each crime and time sentenced for the crime)

If you are serving time for more than one sentence, are you serving your sentences:

At the same time?________ **OR** One after the other? _________

Please answer "Yes" or "No" to the following questions:

Did you or your attorney use an alibi defense at trial? (This means you said you were somewhere else when the crime took place.)

Yes________ No ________

argue that you committed the crime in self-defense (or person)?

s________ No ________

gue that you committed the crime because someone threated u committed the crime?

Yes________ No ________

Did your attorney use a mental illness or brain injury in your defense?

Yes________ No ________

Did your attorney use any other arguments at your trial?

Yes________ No ________

Sample Application (Con't)

If you answered YES to any of the above questions, please describe the evidence your attorney used:

Victim Name(s) and your relation to each:

Were you in a line-up? Yes________ No ________

Were you identified (picked out) in a line up? Yes________ No ________

Were you identified from pictures? Yes________ No ________

Did you give a statement or confession? Yes________ No ________

If yes, describe what you told the police:

PHYSICAL AND BIOLOGICAL EVIDENCE:

Was any physical and/or biological evidence recovered in your case?
Yes________ No ________

Were any bodily fluids or hair samples taken from the victim (examples are vaginal secretions, anal secretions, blood or saliva)

Yes________ No ________

If Yes, what samples did they take?

Were any bodily fluids or hair samples taken from you? (examples are blood, saliva, hair)
Yes________ No ________

If Yes, what samples did they take?

Were bodily fluids or hair found at the crime scene?
Yes________ No ________
If Yes, what was found?

Sample Application (Con't)

What kinds of Scientific Testing were done on the physical/ biological evidence? (DNA, blood type, etc.)

Is there any physical/ biological evidence that could be scientifically tested at this time which you believe would help to prove your innocence? If so, what?

Does any physical/biological evidence still exist? Yes________ No ________
If yes, tell us what it is, where it is, and who has it.

TRIAL

If you did **NOT** go to trial, write "Does not Apply" here: __________________________ and move onto the next section (Guilty Plea). If you **DID** go to trial, please answer these questions:

Trial Case Number:____

Trial Attorney(s); (name, address, phone number):

Prosecuting Attorney(s); (name address, phone number):

Trial Judge Name:

Did you testify? Yes________ No ________

Did the victim(s) testify? Yes________ No ________

GUILTY PLEA

If you did **NOT** plead guilty, please write "Does not Apply" here: ___________________ and move onto the next section (APPEALS). If you **DID** plead guilty, please answer these questions:

Did you give a statement, make a confession or plead guilty? Yes____No ______
If yes, who did you give the statement to?

Sample Application (Con't)

Explain what you included in your statement:

APPEALS

If you have **NOT** appealed, please write "Does not Apply" here____________________ then move onto the next section (POST-CONVICTION MOTIONS). If you **DID** appeal, please answer these questions:

How many appeals have you filed? Please list and include which courts they were filed in.

Names, addresses, and phone numbers of lawyers who handled (or are handling your appeal):

Names, addresses, and phone number of prosecutors for your appeal:

Name of judge(s) who decided your appeal(s) (please indicate in which court and dates decided).

Do you have any pending appeals? Yes________ No ________
If yes, please list.

POST-CONVICTION MOTIONS

Did you file any post-conviction motions? Yes________ No ________

If yes, what motions (Example: petition for habeas corpus or a 3.850 motion) and what issues were raised?

Were they filed in state or federal court?

Name of Judge(s) who decided your post-conviction motions and dates decided:

Do you have any pending Post-Conviction Motions? If so, please list type, date Filed, and in which court.

Sample Application (Con't)

CASE MATERIALS

(Check all the documents that you can provide us with. **Please DO NOT SEND any documents at this time, we cannot return your documents.)**

i. Hearing Transcript(s) ___ii. Trial Transcript(s) ___________________

iii. Police Report(s) _____iv. Laboratory report (s) ___________________

v. Appellate briefs:

Appellant (Defense) ___Respondent (Prosecution) ___________

vi. Post-Conviction Briefs:

Appellant (Defense) _______Respondent (Prosecution) ___________

vii. Are there any friends or family members who have information regarding your case? (Include name, relationship, address, and phone number)

Please provide us with any additional information that you feel would be helpful:

PLEASE READ BEFORE SIGNING

I hereby authorize the students, staff, and volunteer attorneys working with the [insert name of Innocence Program] to research my case. This includes, but is not limited to, communication with my previous attorneys, probation and parole officers, The Department of Corrections, witnesses, and prosecuting attorneys. I understand that the initial investigation is conducted by students, who are not attorneys and do not represent me. I understand the [Program] may at any time decide that the further investigation into my case is not warranted. I understand that in some cases, the [Program] may seek a volunteer lawyer to represent me.

I also authorize the release of any information to students, staff, and volunteer attorneys working with the [insert name of Innocence Program] on my case. This includes, but is not limited to, the release of court transcripts, post-conviction motions, correctional records, laboratory results, police reports, and other legal files. I understand that the attorney-client relationship is not created by the clinic investigating my case or by my case being held on a wait list for an extended period of time.

Date:_________________

Signature:______________________________________

Print Name: ____________________________________

Please Send To: [Address of Innocence Program]

Release Form

Dear [Name]:

By signing this release form, you are giving the University of Miami Innocence Clinic permission to research your case further by obtaining court documents, laboratory results, police records, and other information we may need. We will need this permission if and when we are able to help you. Also, we must know if there is currently a lawyer or group reviewing the case for you.

This form allows the Clinic to speak with persons associated with your case. If there are persons that you do *not* want us to contact, please list them on this form.

We are not consenting to provide you with representation and we recommend that you obtain legal counsel if you are able.

We are not attorneys, but are law students who research claims of actual innocence. Thank you for your patience and you will hear from us if and when we are able to assist you.

Sincerely,

[Name of Innocence Program]

[Address]

[Email]

Print Name:______________________________

Signature:________________________________

Date:____________________________________

Sample Letter Confirming Receipt of Application

[Date]

[Name]

[Address]

Re: Receipt of Application Confirmation

Dear [Defendant's Name]:

The purpose of this letter is to confirm the receipt of your Application for Assistance. The [insert name of Innocence Program]'s request for your Application is not a guarantee that the [Program] has agreed to accept your case.

The [insert name of Innocence Program] realizes that time is of the utmost importance, and will review your Application as quickly as time permits. The Clinic reviews applications in the order they are received.

While it is impossible to predict an exact time frame, it may take several weeks or even months for a screening decision to be made concerning your case. [insert name of Innocence Program] kindly asks that you do not send any additional documents until the [Program] requests them.

The [Program] appreciates your patience in this matter, and assures you we will put forth our best effort to provide you with whatever assistance is possible.

Sincerely,

[Name of Innocence Program]

[Address]

[Email]

Sample Denial Request Form

This form must be filled out completely and sent to all supervisors and approved by at least one supervisor before a case may be denied. Please circle yes or no whether your team has performed the task listed. If your answer is no, space is provided to explain why the task was not performed. You may use extra space if needed. At the end of the denial form there is space provided for your denial narrative. In this area you should explain your reasons for recommending a denial.

Client name:

DC#

Address:

Your name:

Other students working on this case:

Date:

1) Have you obtained the trial transcripts? Yes No
   a. If no, why not?

2) Have you obtained all appellate transcripts? Yes No
   a. If no, why not?

3) Have you obtained all post-conviction documents? Yes No
   a. If no, why not?

Sample Denial Request Form (Con't)

4) Have you obtained all reports (police or expert, etc.)? Yes No
   a. If no, why not?

5) Have you carefully read any transcripts or reports in your possession? Yes No
   a. If no, why not?

6) Have you outlined the above? Yes No
   a. If no, why not?

7) Have you spoken to all previous attorneys on the case? Yes No
   a. If no, why not?

8) Have you spoken to your client? Yes No
   a. If no, why not?

9) Have you spoken to all family and friends listed on the application or provided to you by your client or from other sources? Yes No
   a. If no, why not?

Sample Denial Request Form (Con't)

10) Have you spoken to any possible witnesses who might recant? Yes No
    a. If no, why not?

11) Have you spoken to all previous prosecutors on the case? Yes No
    a. If no, why not?

12) Have you done legal research on this case? Yes No
    a. If no, why not?

13) Have you made a procedural timeline and a fact timeline? Yes No
    a. If no, why not?

14) Please state what efforts you have made to determine whether biological evidence exists in this case?

Sample Denial Request Form (Con't)

15) Please list any other investigation you have done in order to find newly discovered evidence (if outside the time window) or investigation you have done to raise claims in a post-conviction motion.

16) Please provide a narrative to support a denial in this case:

Your Signature: ___________________________

Sample Retainer Agreement

[Date]

[Name]

[Address]

Re: Confirmation of Engagement

Dear [defendant's name]:

The purpose of this letter is to confirm, based on your Application for Assistance dated[insert date] and other information provided to us, that the [insert name of Innocence Program] will represent you in [describe matter]. We will provide the following services: [list services to be provided]

Our expectations of you are: [list any expectations concerning responses to requests for information, etc.]

The [name of Innocence Project Clinic] has not been engaged to provide the following services: [list services that are outside the scope of the representation]

While it is impossible to predict how long it will take to conclude this matter, a general time frame is provided below. Again, this is only an estimate, and the actual time required to conclude this matter may be greater than expected. [Provide a realistic, worst-case estimate of time to be spent on case]

It is expressly agreed and understood by the parties that no promises or guarantees as to the outcome of the case, or of any subsequent legal proceedings arising out of or relating to the case, have been made. It is further understood that the Clinic makes no guarantees for any further representation other than the current proceeding, to wit: [insert services provided]. The [Project Clinic] or the Defendant may cease representation at any time and for any reason.

By signing below you hereby authorize and give express consent for law students to provide you legal representation under the supervision of law faculty.

Sample Retainer Agreement (Con't)

If you have any questions about this information, please contact us. On behalf of the [name of Innocence Project Clinic], we are happy to represent you in this matter.

Very truly yours,

[Director's name]

Agreed, Understood, and Accepted, this __________day of __________, 20__

________________________________ [Defendant's name]

Sample Third Party Letter

[Date]

[Address]

Re: Request for Legal Assistance

Dear [Name]:

Thank you for your correspondence in regards to inmate [Name]. Unfortunately, due to ethical rules governing lawyers, we can only assist inmates who contact us directly and ask for our assistance. Please ask the inmate to directly contact us and request our assistance with a brief fact summary of his case. Only then can we determine whether the case is one that meets the criteria for our [Program].

Sincerely,

[Name of Innocence Program]

[Address]

[Email]

Sample Fax Cover Sheet

Fax

[Address] [Name of Innocence Program]

[Telephone number]

[Fax number]

[Email]

Fax

To:	[Correctional Officer]	From:	[Insert name of Innocence Program]
Fax:	[Insert Fax # of Correctional Institution]	Pages:	[Insert page total]
Phone:	[Insert Phone # of Correctional Institution]	Date:	Today's Date
Re:	[Insert inmate name] – Phone Interview]	cc:	

Comments: This letter is a confirmation that a phone interview with inmate [name and DC#] is scheduled for [insert time]. on [day, date]. The attorney conducting the interview is [insert name and bar # of supervising attorney] We will be calling the [name of correctional institution] at [time told to call] at the contact number given to us

PLEASE BE ADVISED THAT ALL INFORMATION DISCUSSED DURING THE PHONE INTERVIEW IS PROTECTED BY ATTORNEY-CLIENT PRIVILEGE. PLEASE ENSURE THAT THE INMATE IS PROVIDED WITH A NON-MONITORED AND NON-RECORDED PHONE LINE AND THAT THE INMATE IS PROVIDED PRIVACY FOR THE PHONE CALL.

Thank you for your attention in this matter.

[Name of Innocence Program] [Address]

[Email]

Sample Public Records Request

[Date]

[Name of County] Clerk of Court

ATTN: Official Records

Re: Subject:

Date of Birth:

Charge:

Circuit Case #:

To Whom it May Concern:

Pursuant to [insert applicable law], we request copies of public records regarding the cases referenced above.

We are specifically requesting that your office provide **an evidence log or inventory list describing the physical evidence from these cases that remains at your office**. In the event that your physical search does not yield any of the above requested items, we ask that your agency provide us with **any and all destruction orders** as proof that such evidence no longer exists.

Please contact me via fax; email at [email address]; or telephone for more information or with an invoice.

We thank you in advance for your time and assistance in this matter.

Sincerely,

[Name of Innocence Program]

Sample Document Subpoena

IN THE [INSERT NAME OF COURT]

CASE NO. [INSERT CASE NUMBER]

SUBPOENA OF NON-PARTY – DUCES TECUM
(Records may be mailed in lieu of appearance)

[NAME OF DEFENDANT],

Petitioner,

v.

STATE OF [NAME OF STATE],

Respondent.

________________________________/

TO: **Records Custodian**

[Insert Address]

YOU ARE HEREBY COMMANDED to provide the [insert name of Innocence Program] c/o [name of director], at [insert address], by [insert date] with the documents listed in Schedule "A" attached hereto.

Sample Document Subpoena (Con't)

These items will be inspected and may be copied at that time. You will not be required to surrender the original items. You have the right to object to the production pursuant to this subpoena at any time before production by giving written notice to the attorney whose name appears on this subpoena.

If you fail to:

(1) appear as specified; or
(2) furnish the records instead of appearing as provided above; or
(3) object to this subpoena,

you may be in contempt of Court. You are subpoenaed by the attorney whose name appears in this subpoena and unless excused from this subpoena by the attorney or the Court, you shall respond to this subpoena as directed.

DATED this ___________day of _________________, 20__.

[NAME OF INNOCENCE PROGRAM]

SUBMITTED TO THE COURT BY:

____

[DIRECTOR'S NAME], ESQUIRE

BAR NO.: [INSERT BAR NO.]

Attorneys for Petitioner

[Insert address]

[Insert telephone number]: Telephone

Case No.: [Insert case number]

Sample Document Subpoena (Con't)

SCHEDULE "A"

Records pertaining to [insert name and Department of Corrections Identification Number (DOC #) of inmate], since [insert date] through the date of this production as follows:

[List the documents below]

1.

2.

3. etc….

Sample Case Summary Memo

Defendant Name: ________________________________

Student : ______________________________________

Date: ____

Crime Alleged: __________________________________

Cast of Characters:

____

____

____

____

____

____

Case Timeline:

____

____

____

____

____

____

Factual Summary:

____

____

____

____

____

Sample Weekly Case Follow-up Memo

Defendant Name: ______________________________

Student: ______________________________

Date: ______________________________

Crime Alleged: ______________________________

Last Action Taken:

____

____

____

____

Every follow-up memo should include:

1. **Actions Taken – document and memorialize any phone calls or interviews, etc. Make sure any documents received or sent is documented in this memo**
2. **To do list**
3. **Are there any deadlines?**
4. **Are there any legal issues that need to be researched?**
5. **What follow-up investigation can be done?**
6. **Students working on case – contact info**
7. **Make clear which student is doing what task – write it down**
8. **Staple a hard copy of the follow up memo on the file**

Weekly Decision

Continue Investigation ____________

Deny _________ **attach supporting Denial Request Form**

CPSIA information can be obtained
at www.ICGtesting.com
Printed in the USA
FFOW04n1738291215
19700FF

9 781600 421846